D0554527

6.50 AC

On the Transition to Socialism

by Paul M. Sweezy
and Charles Bettelheim

New York and London

Library of Congress Catalog Card Number: 72-158924

First Printing

Monthly Review Press
116 West 14th Street, New York, N. Y. 10011
33/37 Moreland Street, London, E.C. 1

Manufactured in the United States of America

Contents

I

BETWEEN CAPITALISM AND SOCIALISM
A Discussion by Paul M. Sweezy and Charles Bettelheim

II

SOME LESSONS OF RECENT HISTORY
Three Essays from *Monthly Review*

Foreword

Part I of this collection comprises an exchange of views between Charles Bettelheim and myself which appeared in *Monthly Review* beginning in October 1968 and ending in October 1971. All but the last piece were published in French under the title *Lettres sur quelques problèmes actuels du socialisme*. (Paris: Maspero, 1970)

Part II contains two editorial articles from *Monthly Review* and the text of a lecture I delivered in Italy in the spring of 1971, which was also originally published in *Monthly Review*.

The first of the two editorial articles, on the first fifty years of Soviet experience, appeared in November 1967 when Leo Huberman and I were editors; the second, discussing the significance of the worker uprising in Poland in December 1970, appeared in February 1971 when Harry Magdoff and I were editors, as we still are. Since the magazine's inception the editors have had an understanding that any collection of essays by either of them may include unsigned editorial articles of appropriate subject matter. The purpose is to make material available to readers in conveniently usable form and does not indicate sole authorship.

—Paul M. Sweezy

October 1971

I
Between Capitalism
and Socialism

Czechoslovakia, Capitalism, and Socialism

by Paul M. Sweezy

The Russians justify their invasion of Czechoslovakia on the grounds that a counter-revolutionary situation was developing and that if they had not intervened Czechoslovakia would have reverted to capitalism and joined the imperialist camp. This position, including support for the invasion, has also been espoused by some other elements of the international Left, notably by Fidel Castro speaking on behalf of the Cuban revolutionary leadership. Most of the Left in the advanced capitalist countries, on the other hand, has argued what might almost be called the opposite thesis, that Czechoslovakia was headed for a genuine form of democratic socialism and that the Soviet intervention had nothing to do with either capitalism or socialism but was aimed at halting the process of democratization which was considered a threat to the authoritarian rule of the Communist Parties throughout the Eastern European bloc.

The weakest part of the Russian argument is the contention that a counter-revolutionary situation was developing. On the contrary, the existing system had been greatly stabilized and strengthened by the popular reforms of the past eight months. These reforms were largely confined to the political superstructure of the system and did not in any way change its basic character. What was threatening was not a counter-

This article appeared in the October 1968 issue of *Monthly Review*.

revolution but a Congress of the Czechoslovak Communist Party which would have endorsed the reforms and firmly entrenched in power the new leadership under which they had been put into effect. These circumstances certainly lend strong support to the view that it was indeed the reforms which were the target of the Soviet invasion, and nothing that has happened since August 21st argues to the contrary.

However, the fact that not a change but a strengthening of the existing system was on the agenda does not mean that Czechoslovakia was not moving in the direction of capitalism. The trend toward capitalism is built into the present system: control of enterprises in the enterprises themselves, coordination through the market, and reliance on material incentives— these three factors, taken together, make inevitable a strong tendency toward an economic order which, whatever one may choose to call it, functions more and more like capitalism.

To be sure, some Marxists hold that no society can be capitalist unless or until private property in the means of production is explicitly legalized. For example, a Fourth International statement rejecting Castro's position on Czechoslovakia states categorically that "the danger of capitalist restoration . . . can only arise from social forces having the capacity to organize themselves sufficiently to impose the re-establishment of capitalist private ownership by force." (*Intercontinental Press*, September 16, p. 766) This is to confuse juridical categories with real relations of production. If enterprises are run by small groups with a view to maximizing profits through production of commodities for the market, you have the essential production and class relations of capitalism. Appropriate juridical forms will develop in due course, but in view of the historical background they will probably not include anything labeled "private property." Nor will this be entirely a matter of ideological deception. Let us recall that Marx wrote more than a hundred years ago with regard to corporations:

Capital, which rests on a socialized mode of production and presupposes a social concentration of means of production and labor powers, is here directly endowed with the form of social capital (capital of directly associated individuals) as distinguished from private capital, and its enterprises assume the form of social enterprises as distinguished from individual enterprises. It is the abolition of capital as private property within the boundaries of capitalist production itself.*

If the old unambiguous concept of individual private property was already so greatly complicated by the rise of the corporation, think how much more complicated it is today in the era of the multinational corporation and massive state ownership. In both Italy and France, for example, the state, directly or through state corporations, owns a large proportion of the means of production—certainly not *private* ownership yet just as certainly a form of *capitalist* ownership. And it is only reasonable to assume that we must expect still other new forms of capitalist ownership in the future.

It is true that in Czechoslovakia the three features mentioned above are far from fully developed: the system is still a mixture of what is often called "market socialism"** and the kind of centralized administrative planning which had its origins in the Soviet Union during the Stalin period and was exported to the other Soviet bloc countries after the Second World War. But what is important is not the exact composition of the present mixture but the direction in which the system is moving, and here there can be no doubt (a) that the weight of the market elements has been growing for at least the last five years and (b) that one of the purposes of the liberalizing

---

* *Capital*, Kerr ed., Vol. 3, p. 616. An error in translation has been corrected.

** The very term "market socialism" is self-contradictory, the market being the central institution of capitalist society and socialism being a society which substitutes conscious control for blind automatism. But this does not mean that the term is inappropriate: the phenomenon which it designates is also self-contradictory. And it is precisely this inner contradiction which impels the market socialist societies toward capitalism. Unfortunately, it must be said that the level of Marxist analysis of these extremely important phenomena is depressingly low, not only in the United States but throughout the international Left. People who have learned the lesson that to understand capitalism one must dig deep below the surface to uncover underlying relationships and processes are content, when it comes to the socialist societies, to deal with appearances only. Much of the blame, of course, must be laid at the door of the socialist societies themselves, all of which without exception have shunned any serious scientific study of their own reality.

reforms of the last eight months has been to remove obstacles to the further streamlining of the Czech economy along market lines.* It is no accident that one of the most prominent and influential figures of this latest period has been Professor Ota Sik who was promoted to the post of Deputy Premier in the Dubcek regime. Next to the Soviet economist Liberman, Sik is perhaps the best known theorist and advocate of market socialism; and he was the principal author of the economic reform program which was adopted and began to be haltingly implemented in 1964.

Since it is Yugoslavia which has gone much farther than any other country in the direction of market socialism, it is to Yugoslavia that one must look if one wants to see where the course adopted by Czechoslovakia is leading. The turn to the market in Yugoslavia dates back to the split with the Cominform in 1948, so that there we have not five years but two decades of experience to learn from. So far one must admit that it is capitalist observers and analysts rather than their socialist counterparts who have shown themselves able to report accurately on Yugoslav developments and to draw the necessary conclusions. Here is a dispatch from Belgrade which appeared on the financial page of the *New York Times* of August 19, 1968:

> Western capital has gained an important foothold in Yugoslavia and is helping turn what was once chiefly an agricultural country into a new industrial state.
>
> Investments by such diverse enterprises as Fiat, the Italian auto giant, and Printing Developments, Inc., of New York City, a subsidiary of Time, Inc., represent both the voracious demands of capital for new outlets and the conscious designs of a Communist state to accept a market economy and most of the trappings.
>
> Conversations with Belgrade officials specializing in economic activities show their firm conviction that this route will be followed by other countries of Eastern Europe.
>
> To them Yugoslavia is a pacesetter in the East as well as a show window for Western capital. Western companies operating here will have enormous competitive advantages once markets open up elsewhere in Eastern Europe.

---

* In *Business Week's* succinct summary, the Dubcek regime "moved to free the press, allow more individual liberties, and apply capitalist techniques to pep up the sluggish Czech economy." (August 24)

Following reforms that shifted control of enterprises from the state to the enterprises themselves and introduced the disciplines of the free market and the incentive of profits, Yugoslavia promulgated an equally revolutionary law a year ago to attract foreign capital.

The law did not come without strong opposition from those fearful that Western capital would dominate the key sectors of the economy.

To guard against this, foreign capital is barred from acquiring more than a 49 percent interest in a Yugoslav enterprise.

Yugoslav companies are controlled by their workers through worker councils, which, in turn, name a board of professionals, such as accountants and production engineers, to manage their plant.

At first foreign companies were reluctant to get involved because the minority stake, they felt, would not give them any direct control over their investment.

At seminars run for Western businessmen here, Yugoslav officials have been at pains to point out that ways can be found around this, for example, by vesting in the foreign investor control over costs of production.

The foreigners are permitted to transfer profits out of the country provided they keep 20 percent on deposit with a Yugoslav bank. They can sell their stake to other foreign companies provided they first offer to sell it back to the Yugoslav company.

The law has produced some dramatic results.

Fiat, which is supplying the technology and most of the equipment for a big Soviet auto plant, put $10 million into a Yugoslav company, Crvena Zastava (Red Flag) that makes Fiat cars under license.

The American company, according to published information here, has gone into a joint venture with Beogradski Graficki Zavod (Belgrade Graphical Printing Company) to do color printing using especially fast, new processing equipment from the United States.

Of course it may be said that all this relates to Yugoslavia and that it doesn't prove that Czechoslovakia is headed in the same direction. True enough: it would undoubtedly be impossible to prove it to the satisfaction of someone who is wedded to another view. The problem of analyzing social reality is always complicated by the fact that new developments which are on the way to becoming predominant arise from small beginnings which can be ignored or pooh-poohed by anyone who chooses to do so. All one can say is that Czechoslovakia has already taken more than a few steps along the road pioneered by the Yugoslavs and in the months before the invasion gave every indication of moving faster in the same direction. Already some deals with foreign companies to build plants in Czechoslovakia had been negotiated (for example, according to *Business Week* of August 31st, ENI, the Italian oil trust, is building a chemical factory in Czechoslovakia); so many foreign businessmen were flocking to Prague that at least one hotel was practically reserved for their occupancy; and insistent, and apparently well founded, stories circulated both in Prague and in Western financial centers that a $500-million loan was in the works to enable the Czechs to import the latest technology and equipment from the West. Maybe all this is of no significance; or maybe the consequences of relying on the market and developing increasingly intimate relations with capitalist countries would be different in Czechoslovakia from what they have been in Yugoslavia. Maybe, but I have yet to see a serious argument supporting any such conclusions.

It should be emphasized here that there is no implication that the Czech reformers—or even the Yugoslavs for that matter—are consciously moving toward capitalism, or that they are being hypocritical and insincere when they say that they are working to achieve democratic socialism. Marxism teaches us not to judge people by their intentions but by their acts and the probable consequences of their acts. The contention is that whoever acts to strengthen the market instead of struggling against the market is, regardless of intentions, promoting capitalism and not socialism.*

Does it follow that because Czechoslovakia was moving toward capitalism, this was the reason for the Soviet intervention? Absolutely not. The truth is that the whole Eastern European bloc, including the Soviet Union, has been and is

---

* The most important (and most neglected) Marxist work on this general range of subjects is E. Preobrazhensky, *The New Economics,* originally published in the Soviet Union in the mid-1920s and recently issued in an English translation (Oxford University Press, 1965). Preobrazhensky was a member of the Left Opposition and was killed in the Stalinist purges. See also the analysis of the Yugoslav system in "Peaceful Transition from Socialism to Capitalism?" *Monthly Review,* Vol. 15, No. 11 (March 1964), pp. 569-590.

moving in the same direction as Yugoslavia and Czechoslovakia. This is the real meaning of the economic reform movement which, in varying degrees and at varying speeds, has involved every member of the bloc. Everywhere, the old system of bureaucratic centralism was running into increasing difficulties. Mass apathy, faltering productivity, economic stagnation—these and other symptoms of impending crisis were visible throughout the region. There were two possible responses. One would have been a cultural revolution in the specific sense that the Chinese have given to that term: an all-out campaign to rouse the masses, to elevate the general level of political consciousness, to revitalize socialist ideals, to give increasing responsibility to the producers themselves at all levels of decision-making. The other response was to rely increasingly on the discipline of the market and the incentive of profit. For reasons which reach far back into the history of the Soviet Union and the Communist movement, there was no one, no party, no group capable of making the first response. The second course was therefore adopted, not because the bureaucracies had any love for the capitalist methods but because they could see no other way to preserve their power and privileges. The price they must pay, whether they know it or not, whether they like it or not, is to put their countries on the road back to essentially capitalist societies.

In his speech of August 23rd on the invasion of Czechoslovakia, Fidel Castro, referring to an article in *Pravda,* said:

It reads as follows: "The CPSU is constantly perfecting the style, the forms, and the methods of the construction of the party and the state. This same work is being carried out in other socialist countries in a tranquil process based on the fundamentals of the socialist system."

But this statement is very interesting. It says: "Unfortunately, discussions concerning economic reform in Czechoslovakia developed on another basis. That discussion centered, on the one hand, around a global criticism of all development proceeding from the socialist economy and, on the other, around the proposal to replace the principles of planning with spontaneous mercantile relations, granting a broad field of action to private capital."

Does this, by chance, mean that the Soviet Union is also going to curb certain currents in the field of economy that are in favor of putting increasingly greater emphasis on mercantile relations and on the effects of spontaneity in those relations, and those which have even been defending the desirability of the market and of prices based on that market? Does it mean that the Soviet Union is becoming aware of the need to halt those currents? More than one article in the imperialist press has referred jubilantly to those currents that also exist within the Soviet Union.

I dare say that Fidel knows as well as anyone else that *Pravda's* article was intended to score a point and not to signalize a fundamental change in Soviet policy. The fact is that the decadent bureaucracies of the Soviet bloc have tried the only kind of centralized planning they can conceive of and have proved that it doesn't meet the needs and expectations of their peoples. They have no alternative but to turn once again to the methods of capitalism. And in so doing, they have entered on a one-way street which, however long the journey, has only one destination.

No, the Soviet invasion of Czechoslovakia was not intended to check the drift to capitalism. That proceeds in both countries and will continue unless or until something far more drastic occurs than a liberal reform program of the kind that has been under way in Czechoslovakia these last eight months. What the leaders of the Soviet Union feared—and had every reason to fear—were two threats, one to their personal interests and the other to the interests of the national ruling stratum which they represent.

The threat to their personal interests was simple. The liberal reforms in Czechoslovakia were extremely popular in that country, and for obvious reasons. If you have been kept in prison for a long time, your first objective is to get out, not to change the system. That was essentially the situation of the Czechoslovak people: they wanted most of all to get out of prison, and that meant getting rid of the Novotny regime with all its repressive and repugnant features. They succeeded with remarkable ease. The Communist Party turned out to be surprisingly responsive to the popular mood; the old-line leadership was caught unawares and swept out of power without even being able to put up a struggle. To the rulers of the Soviet

Union and the other bloc countries, whose people are also in prison (and in the case of the Soviet Union have been there much longer), this could not but be a terrifying example. If Novotny and company could be unceremoniously kicked out, so could they. From their point of view, it was therefore essential not only to tighten up controls in their own countries but show that Czechoslovakia could not get away with it after all. From their point of view, this consideration alone was probably enough to justify the invasion.

But there was an added reason which particularly affected the Soviet leadership, occupying, as it does, the dominant position in the bloc as a whole. With the growing importance of the market throughout the region, the magnetic force of the more powerful market economies of the West also grows. Once profit and efficiency at the plant and enterprise levels have been elevated to the status of supreme values, managements will inevitably strive for closer association with those who are most advanced and proficient in putting these values into practice. The demand for more trade, more technology, more finance, and finally more investment from the advanced capitalist countries is bound to increase. Yugoslavia shows this process with crystal clarity—and also how it leads to the weaker country falling increasingly under the domination of the stronger. In terms of the bloc as a whole, what we are talking about here are very powerful centrifugal forces which, if unchecked, will result in an accelerating process of disintegration. For the ruling stratum in the Soviet Union, of course, this represents a serious danger. The bloc has been structured—economically, politically, and militarily—to serve its group and national interests. Czechoslovakia and East Germany, for example, as relatively advanced industrial regions, have been assigned economic roles which are tailored to the needs of the Soviet economy. (To what extent these relationships are also exploitative is important but not crucial to the problem with which we are presently concerned.) And it is obvious that the Soviet leadership considers the continuation in force of the Warsaw Pact to be essential to its military security. Under these circumstances, it is easy to understand why the men in the Kremlin are prepared to use what-

ever means may be necessary to hold the bloc together. And
since their combined economic and political power is being
constantly eroded and is no longer sufficient to do the job,
they have felt obliged to have recourse to naked armed force.

In the final analysis, then, the invasion of Czechoslovakia
was a sign of Soviet weakness in the face of a growing crisis
in the bloc as a whole. Can it succeed? In the short run,
undoubtedly. Liberalization in Czechoslovakia has been slowed
down and may be halted altogether for a while; the centrifugal
forces tending to disintegrate the bloc have been checked. But
in the longer run, military force is totally incapable of coping
with economic and political problems. It was these problems
that brought on the crisis, and they will just as surely bring on
new and greater crises in the future.

In the meantime, orthodox Moscow-oriented Communism
has suffered a disaster from which it may never recover. As
far as Europe is concerned, a letter received the other day from
an old Austrian friend summed up the situation very well:

I have belonged, as you doubtless know, to that small minority
of left-wing socialists who could not bring themselves to cut their
last ties (ideological as well as political) to the "glorious" Russian
party. Sometime, somehow, one continued hoping, a radical shake-
up would occur and the old Leninist traditions could come to life
once again.

It would be foolish to maintain such hopes today. Yester-
day Ernst Fischer [leading intellectual in the Austrian CP] called
upon the Left to dissociate itself from the men in the Kremlin,
and to take its own way. I wonder whether the Western Communist Parties will be able to heed Fischer's advice. If they don't,
they would, in my opinion, face slow but certain extinction.

If this assessment is accurate, the Czech crisis marks the
beginning of the end of Moscow's political and ideological
influence in the advanced capitalist countries. Either the Communist Parties recognize it and try to adjust to it, or they go
under. Given their histories, it is doubtful whether they can
successfully adjust. But either way, the era of Moscow-orienta-
tion is nearing the end.

Outside the advanced capitalist world the impact will be
less dramatic—but only because there the orthodox Communist

Parties have long been withering away, and new revolutionary forces looking for inspiration to China or (in Latin America) to Cuba have come to the fore.

As far as Cuba is concerned, Fidel's speech condoning the invasion will hardly enhance the prestige of the Cuban Revolution. However, it must be said that it is by no means fair to judge the speech by that part alone. Most of three and a half newspaper pages it took up in *Granma* (August 25) were devoted to a shrewd and biting critique of the kind of socialism practiced in Eastern Europe, and a castigation of Soviet world policies. For the rest, Cuba will be judged in the international revolutionary movement less by what its leaders say than by what policies they put into practice inside and outside Cuba. And in this respect their record has been and continues to be remarkably good for a small country, relatively isolated and subjected to the full weight of a vicious imperialist blockade.

Finally, it may well turn out that the biggest gainer from the Czechoslovak crisis will be China which denounced the invasion as it deserved to be denounced without falling into the naïvetés of the theory which saw Czechoslovakia as headed for some kind of a democratic socialist utopia. There is much in China's analysis of the current international scene which *Monthly Review* has never been able to accept—e.g., the treatment of the Soviet Union's course in world affairs as though it were the sole responsibility of a "revisionist renegade clique" rather than the product of five decades of Soviet history, and the labeling of all the countries of the Soviet bloc as already fully capitalist rather than societies in transition toward capitalism: these are typical Chinese errors which often lead to wrong estimates and conclusions. Nevertheless, in the Czechoslovak case, the Chinese analysis, as expounded for example by Commentator (generally thought to be a high official of the Chinese Communist Party) in the *People's Daily* of August 23rd, is clear and to the point:

That the Soviet revisionist renegade clique has flagrantly set in motion its armed forces is the outcome of the extremely acute contradictions within the whole modern revisionist bloc. It is the result of the extremely acute contradictions between United States imperialism and Soviet modern revisionism in their struggle for control of Eastern Europe. It is the outcome of the collaboration between the United States and the Soviet Union in their vain attempt to re-divide the world. For a long time there have existed profound contradictions and bitter strife between the Soviet revisionist renegade clique and the revisionist cliques of the Eastern European countries. The Khrushchev revisionist renegade clique, ever since it rose to power, has most shamefully made one dirty deal after another with United States imperialism. Following the example of the Soviet revisionists, the Czechoslovak revisionist renegade clique want to follow in their footsteps, throwing themselves into the lap of United States imperialism. However, the Soviet revisionists regard Eastern Europe as their own sphere of influence and forbid the Czechoslovak revisionists to have direct collaboration with United States imperialism. (Hsinhua release, August 23)

The world revolutionary movement, especially in the underdeveloped countries, is more likely to be impressed with the truths of this statement than with its exaggerations. After all, to convey the truth it may sometimes be necessary to exaggerate.

On the Transition Between Capitalism and Socialism
by Charles Bettelheim

I read with great interest your article on "Czechoslovakia, Capitalism, and Socialism." It contains many important and accurate statements—especially those in which you say that the Czech reforms were strengthening the existing system, and stress the fact that what was involved was a new step along the road of capitalism (you say: "in the direction of capitalism"). Your denunciation of the confusion of "juridical categories" with "real relations of production" is similarly an indispensable correction. This applies equally to your remark that capitalist ownership is not necessarily "private" ownership (personally, I think that it may be more appropriate in this context to speak of "individual" ownership, since capitalist ownership as a social relationship is always "private" ownership—that of a class—even if it assumes a "social" juridical form; I think that when Marx speaks of "the abolition of capital as private property, within the boundaries of capitalist production itself," his target is precisely "private" ownership *in the juridical sense*). Some of your conclusions also strike me as very correct, particularly your statement that "in the final analysis . . . the invasion of Czechoslovakia was a sign of Soviet weakness in the face of a growing crisis in the bloc as a whole."

Your article, however, also contains elaborations which strike me as erroneous, and which I would like to discuss. I shall limit myself to two basic problems: (1) the problem of the nature of socialism, and (2) the problem of the roots of the

15

trends toward the restoration of capitalism (hence, of the origin of this restoration where it has already clearly taken place, as in Yugoslavia).

I begin with the second point.

Your thesis seems essentially the following: the trend toward the restoration of capitalism has its "origin" in the role attributed to the *market,* in the reliance on *material incentives,* and in *organizational forms* (what you, on p. 4 above, call control of enterprises "in the enterprises themselves").

I think, however, that this list only designates "secondary facts"—*indices or results,* and not the *decisive factor.*

In my opinion, the *decisive factor*—i.e., the *dominant factor* —is not *economic* but *political.*

This decisive political factor (the importance of which you unfortunately appear to deny in the last pages of your article) results from the fact that the proletariat (Soviet or Czech) *has lost its power to a new bourgeoisie,* with the result that the revisionist leadership of the Communist Party of the Soviet Union is today the instrument of this new bourgeoisie.

It is impossible to *explain* the invasion of Czechoslovakia, the international political line of the USSR (the character of its relations with the United States and with China), or the "reforms" and the results toward which they tend (the full development of the "market," and the economic, political, and ideological domination over the masses made possible by market forms), unless it is recognized that the proletariat is no longer in power.

To list as the primary factor—as you do—not class relations (the existence of a bourgeoisie which "collectively" owns the means of production) but *market* relations is due, it seems to me, to an error in principle, and leads to a number of other errors.

The error in principle is the very one you denounce at the end of the note on p. 5 above; there you say that in order to understand the nature of a mode of production (or of a social formation), "one must dig deep below the surface to uncover underlying relationships and processes." But to put emphasis on the existence of a "market" (and therefore also on the existence of money and prices) in defining the nature of a social formation, means precisely to put emphasis on the *surface,* on what is immediately "apparent"—it is consequently a failure to come to grips with underlying relationships. These exist at the level of production, i.e., at the level of basic social relationships. It is the system of these relationships that produces determined *effects* (economic, political, ideological) on the agents of production. One of these essential effects may be to *divide* the agents into *social* classes and place these classes in *determined objective relationships* (of domination, exploitation, etc.).

The practice (economic, political, ideological) of the *agents* and particularly of the political leaders can be understood only in terms of the place they occupy within the system of social relationships.

The error in principle—putting emphasis on surface phenomena,* on the existence of a market, money, and prices (which existed also before the Twentieth Congress and which exist in all the socialist countries), and on the practice of the leadership with respect to the "market" (a practice which precisely should be *explained*)—leads inevitably to other errors.

The most serious of these errors concerns the problem of the nature of socialism; I shall therefore deal at some length with a few of your formulations.

You very correctly condemn the use of the term "market socialism," but your reasons for this condemnation strike me as theoretically inadequate.

It is correct to condemn the use of the term "market socialism" chiefly because this term places a one-sided emphasis on the existence of market forms in socialist society. It is here that this term reveals its ideological character; it indicates an ideology which favors a considerable development of market

---

* I think that in the analysis of a social formation two kinds of "errors" (i.e., of ideological approaches) are readily made. One is to "limit" the "analysis" to *juridical forms* (this is the error you denounce); the other is to "limit" the "analysis" to *economic forms* (this is the error which you make, and which is also present in any discourse on political economy concerned only with *forms*: exchange, money, prices, market, etc.). *In both cases no true analysis takes place,* since *the emphasis is precisely on forms,* i.e., on what is "manifest," whereas analysis must reach the "underlying" elements which the manifest content dissimulates (while at the same time "revealing" them).

relationships, when in fact such a development (which is possible only under the domination of a bourgeoisie) leads to the full restoration of capitalism.

But your criticisms are of a different nature.

On the one hand, you denounce not the *development*, beyond a certain point, of market relationships, but the very *existence* of market relationships; moreover, you *isolate* this existence and therefore disregard the *social and political conditions* which make the full development of market relationships possible. You thereby grant a "privileged" status to these *forms*, which are posed without reference to the conditions without which it is impossible to give a "description" of their significance. In doing this—and here I repeat the statement I have made earlier—you grant a privileged status to a secondary fact, a surface fact, and obscure what is essential and primary: the basic social relationships, the class relationships.

On the other hand—and this follows from the preceding point—your argument, in my opinion, rests on an important confusion. You say that the term "market socialism" is "contradictory." Formally this is obviously not an argument, since all reality is contradictory. The only problem then is to know whether the verbal expression of a reality and of the contradictions which characterize it *is adequate or not*—i.e., whether these contradictions are *analyzed* in scientific terms or only *shown* in ideological terms.

With respect to the contradiction which forms the subject of this discussion and which you designate as one which assumes the form of a contradiction between "plan" and "market," the very fact that this is a contradiction in practice indicates that it is neither a "verbal" contradiction nor an "ideological contradiction" (in the sense of a contradiction inherent in a certain ideological "conception" of socialism), but that it *expresses,* in *terms that are still ideological,* a *real* and effective contradiction.

Moreover—and I believe that here lies the root of our disagreement—the contradiction "plan"-"market" designates an essential contradiction in socialism viewed as a *transitional* or *passing* form; this contradiction is the *surface effect* caused by a deeper contradiction, by the basic contradiction in the transitional form which is obviously situated at the level of the production relationships and productive forces. In certain cases this surface contradiction becomes the principal contradiction, but it can never be correctly dealt with if it is not viewed in relation to the structure of the production relationships and the productive forces.

The preceding means that the contradiction between "market" and "plan" will continue throughout the transition from capitalism to communism.

What characterizes socialism as opposed to capitalism is not (as your article suggests) the existence or non-existence of market relationships, money, and prices, but the existence of the domination of the proletariat, of the dictatorship of the proletariat. It is through the exercise of this dictatorship in all areas—economic, political, ideological—that market relations can be progressively eliminated by means of *concrete* measures adapted to *concrete situations and conjunctures*. This elimination cannot be "decreed" or "proclaimed." It requires political *strategy* and political *tactics*. When these are lacking, the finest proclamations may lead to the opposite of one's stated (and hoped for) goal.

The notion of a "direct" and "immediate" abolition of market relations is as utopian and dangerous as the notion of the "immediate abolition" of the state, and is *similar in nature*: it disregards the specific characteristics (i.e., the *specific contradictions*) of the period of transition which constitutes the period of the building of socialism.

The *trend* of the evolution at the level of *forms* (the development or retreat of market forms) is an *index* of the evolution of social relationships, but it is no more than an *index*. To "limit" oneself to this index—without elucidating the movement of the contradictions that determine this evolution—may therefore be completely misleading. In certain circumstances the proletariat which has assumed power may also be forced into strategic or tactical *retreats* on the economic front.

It goes without saying that in order for these *retreats* not to be transformed into *defeats* the first condition is that they be clearly understood as such and not understood (and "presented") as "victories," for the ultimate aim is the complete elimination of market relationships; there can be no doubt that this is possible only with the disappearance of the state, and this can be achieved only through the establishment of communism on a world scale.

If in the Soviet Union the restoration of bourgeois domination is accompanied by an *extension* of the role of the market, this is evidently because this domination cannot be complete ("accomplished") except through the full restoration of market relationships; this is, moreover, the reason why this restoration can be understood only as an effect, as a secondary phenomenon, and not as a primary phenomenon.

Another error (and it is a "transformation" of the preceding one), it seems to me, is the assertion that the existence of the "market/plan contradiction" is an impelling force leading toward the restoration of capitalism (this is stated in your note cited above).

In reality, at the level of forms this contradiction is not an impelling force leading toward anything. *Everything depends on the manner in which it is dealt with,* and this manner depends itself on class relations, including those existing at the ideological level.

I wish to add that I consider it useful to present these criticisms because the formulations you advance—and which you are not alone in advancing (they are found especially in the speeches of Fidel and the writings of Che)—result objectively in producing *effects of ideological obscurantism.*

These formulations in effect mask the essential problem of socialism, that of power, the defense of which under certain conditions may even require, as I have recalled earlier, retreats on the economic front (e.g., the NEP). If your formulations were taken literally, Lenin, in favoring the NEP—i.e., in "strengthening the market"— supposedly "promoted capitalism."

The effect of ideological obscurantism stemming from the formulation I am criticizing manifests itself particularly in your analysis of the "economic reforms." Reading this analysis, one has the impression that at the time they decided on these reforms, the Soviet leaders supposedly could have made a "choice" between two "techniques": "One would have been a cultural revolution in the specific sense that the Chinese have given to that term. . . . The other response was to rely increasingly on the discipline of the market and the incentive of profit." (p. 9 above)

But what is involved here is not a "choice" between two techniques that would enable the economy to "progress," but a *line of demarcation* between two political courses, between two classes.

To be sure, the problem that remains to be solved *on the historical level* is that of the concrete process which made possible the reconstitution in the Soviet Union of a powerful bourgeois class and its accession to political power. The Twentieth Congress as a matter of fact could not have had its particular content or effects if there had not *already* existed social relationships unfavorable to the dictatorship of the proletariat. This is also a good indication of the fact that the development of these social relationships was not "determined" by the development of the market, but on the contrary was *anterior* to it.

On the theoretical level, on the other hand (and here too I find myself in disagreement with your article), the declarations of the Communist Party of China concerning the Cultural Revolution, its objectives and methods, clearly elucidate the *ideological* and *political* conditions that must be realized before the threat of a bourgeois restoration can be successfully opposed. These declarations, to be sure, are not only theoretical; they contain also numerous *concrete* discussions of the *concrete* conditions in China. These declarations therefore cannot be "applied" mechanically, but their theoretical core has universal value.

I will add that in given historical circumstances the effect of ideological obscurantism mentioned earlier is increased through an effect of displacement. This occurs when the ideological positions which provoke this effect of obscurantism "feed" a political practice. Such, I think, is the case of the political practice of the Cuban leadership (which I consider it necessary to discuss briefly at this point).

If this leadership attaches so much "importance" to problems of market relationships—to the point of making them the "center" of its ideological conception and political practice—this cannot be the result only of a subjective "error." In my opinion, this is the effect of an ideology and a political line which concentrate all power in the hands of a ruling group, and which therefore do not create the necessary conditions—ideological, organizational, and political—for the democratic exercise of proletarian power.

On the one hand, this political practice has a class significance which cannot be analyzed here; I shall say only that it is related to political domination by a "radicalized" section of the petty bourgeoisie. On the other hand, it produces *necessary consequences*—i.e., consequences that force themselves of necessity on a government that "appeals" to socialism.

One of these consequences is precisely an *ideological displacement*: the *identification* of socialism *not with the dictatorship of the proletariat* (consequently with the power of the laboring masses, with the domination of the Marxist-Leninist ideology, with the practice by the revolutionary leadership of a mass line, etc.) but with the "disappearance" of market relationships.

This "disappearance" is evidently purely *mythical,* for it cannot take place under the given concrete conditions which include of necessity the existence of money and prices, so that the fact of "denying" this existence leads to the opposite of the desired aim—notably to the development of a black market. In spite of speeches and repression, the effects of real relationships always end by imposing themselves.

The *substitution* of the myth of the "disappearance" of the market, money, etc., for the necessary dictatorship of the proletariat obviously involves a *political line*—a line corresponding to precise social forces and a precise ideology.

The speeches of the Cuban leadership,* especially Fidel's

---

* Political *analysis,* of course, must never interpret ideological speeches literally. Here, too, *analysis* takes place only when one goes beyond the surface of the speech, consequently beyond its *manifest* "meaning," in order to uncover its *latent* meaning, the meaning which the terms of the speech at one and the same time dissimulate and reveal. Such an elucidation must first of all locate those passages of the speech in

speech of August 23, 1968, confirm this: what the Cuban leaders "criticize" in the developments which took place in the Soviet Union and the Warsaw Pact countries is not the restoration of a bourgeois dictatorship, or even the absence of proletarian democracy and a mass line, but only *certain* effects of a class domination which, precisely, *remain unmentioned.*

---

which "masking" occurs; such passages constitute "critical points." These are naturally of various kinds, depending on the ideologies involved; but they present themselves frequently in the form of "myths," which are signs of the *unthought,* of obsessive and passionate themes that must be analyzed, so that a meaning may be uncovered other than the apparent one—a meaning which is no more "present" in the consciousness of the author of the speech than in the consciousness of the listener or the reader who naively responds to the literal meaning.

In the speeches of the Cuban leadership, especially since 1964, these obsessive and mythical themes are constituted by the "market," "money," "prices," the "calculations" of economists, etc. On analysis, these themes appear to be the "signifiers" by means of which very different "signifieds" are "repressed" (and "represented"): whatever "threatens" a highly concentrated political power which has raised itself above the masses. These "threats" (thought of as "threats against socialism") present themselves in the manifest form of the "market," "money," etc.; but beyond this form they "represent" the masses, their labor (which must be properly *accounted* for, if this labor is not to be arbitrarily wasted), their aspirations, their always possible spontaneous movements (the speech of August 23, 1968, which denounces precisely the "spontaneity" of market relationships is quite "significant").

It is the presence or absence of these unthought "signifieds" which fuels the vehemence of the speeches against money and market relationships.

In real political practice it is clearly possible to distinguish between a proletarian practice and a non-proletarian practice.

The former is constantly preoccupied with "financial strictness," stable and declining prices, with raising the standard of living of the masses by lowering the prices of widely used consumer goods. This was one of the concerns of Soviet policy until the Twentieth Congress. This is the constant concern of Chinese policy. Such a concern is not "fetishism"; it stems from respect for the labor furnished by the masses, and for their rights.

The second practice is indifferent to inflation or shortages, and conceals this indifference by speaking contemptuously of "economic, monetary, and financial" problems. This contempt, however, is in actual fact contempt for the labor of the masses and their rights. It has therefore *the same character* as contempt for proletarian democracy, for the free expression of opinions by the masses. If this second kind of contempt cannot be expressed but must be *repressed,* the first kind, however, may assume an *ideological form* enabling it to affirm itself openly. This form thus reflects a *dougle signified*—one "thought" in ideological terms (i.e., in reality not thought), the other strictly "unthought."

These effects are not mentioned because the Cuban leaders themselves do not *see* them. They do not see them because their ideology makes it impossible for *this crucial problem* even "to present itself" to them. In their eyes, the "dictatorship of the proletariat" is "assured" by the existence of certain "forms" (a certain juridical form of ownership, a certain organizational form of the Party, a certain form of expression, etc.) and not by concrete social and political relationships.

If I have insisted on emphasizing the ideological effects of the central role which you attribute to the "market/plan" contradiction, this is because the fact of granting such a role to this contradiction (which is no more than a contradiction at the level of *forms*) *makes it possible, in ideological representation, for this contradiction to occupy the place occupied, in Marxist analysis, by the fundamental bourgeoisie-proletariat contradiction.*

Under given political conditions, this displacement also makes it possible to mask the real problems of the transition from capitalism to socialism, since these problems involve above all the development of the proletariat-bourgeoisie contradiction. This "displacement" consequently produces at one and the same time *ideological* effects and *political* effects.

—*Translated by Fred Ehrenfeld*

A Reply
by Paul M. Sweezy

At the outset I want to thank Professor Bettelheim for his carefully considered critique. It continues and in some respects goes beyond his important work *La transition vers l'économie socialiste* (Paris: Maspero, 1968) which, as he says in that book's preface, is devoted to a "group of theoretical and practical questions which become increasingly important from year to year but on which there are very few studies."*

There is one crucial respect in which it seems to me that the above critique goes beyond the book. Let me quote again from the book's preface:

> What lends unity to the chapters which follow is that they constitute the beginning of a new critical reflection bearing on problems which are currently described as those of the "transition toward socialism." It will be seen that this expression is far from being adequate to the reality which it pretends to describe. What it does is to evoke a "forward movement" of which the destination, more or less assured, would be socialism. Now what in fact is described in this way is an historical period which can be more accurately characterized as being that of "the transition *between* capitalism and socialism." Such a period does not lead to socialism in a linear fashion; it may lead there, but it can also lead to renewed forms of capitalism, notably to state capitalism.

---

* I had not yet read the book when I wrote the piece on Czechoslovakia. If I had, I could perhaps have expressed my thoughts in a way which would not have given rise to some of the misunderstandings noted below.

That this possibility exists appears progressively in the course of the chapters which follow; but it is not made the object of an explicit formulation before Chapter 6 [the last in the book]; and in addition the terminology employed reflects this conclusion only partially.

What are called chapters in the book are all previously published essays, and their arrangement is roughly chronological, covering the years 1964-1967, with the last (Chapter 6) having been written more than a year after any of the others (both Chapter 6 and the preface are dated August 1967). From these facts it seems that we can deduce that up to a few years ago Bettelheim still held what I think can be called the traditional Marxist view that the transition from capitalism to socialism is a one-way street. By 1967 he had altered this to allow the *possibility* of a regression to capitalism. And by the end of 1968 (the above critique is dated December 15), he states without qualification that a new bourgeoisie is in power in the Soviet Union—also in Czechoslovakia and by implication in the other Warsaw Pact countries—and that "the Communist Party of the Soviet Union is the instrument of this new bourgeoisie." What was considered a possibility in 1967 is thus adjudged a *fait accompli* in 1968.

Let me hasten to add that in tracing this evolution of Bettelheim's position on the character of the transition period, I intend no criticism. Quite the contrary. Under the stimulus of the polemics between China and the Soviet Union plus personal observation in Yugoslavia, the editors of *Monthly Review* had concluded as early as 1964 that the transition period is a two-way street.* But, as the editorial made clear, we were not satisfied with the Chinese treatment of what had happened in Yugoslavia, and we felt that there was a crying need for more extensive and more profound analysis of what is evidently a crucially important problem. Fortunately, there are few if any Marxists better qualified than Charles Bettelheim to help fill this need. The appearance of his book and the further extension of his ideas along the lines of the above critique should set the stage for a lively and fruitful discussion.

First, then, an attempt to clear away certain misunder-

* "Peaceful Transition from Socialism to Capitalism?" *Monthly Review*, Vol. 15, No. 11 (March 1964), pp. 569-590.

standings. If I read him correctly, Bettelheim attributes to me the view that the very existence of "market relationships, money, and prices" is incompatible with socialism and makes impossible a transition to socialism; and a large part of his critique is devoted to an attack on this position. The evidence on which he relies is apparently the footnote on p. 5 above. On re-reading the footnote I can see how it might lend itself to this interpretation, though it certainly did not occur to me at the time of writing. In any case, I want now to make clear that I never had the slightest intention or inclination to espouse the view Bettelheim attributes to me. The view I do hold is that market relationships (which of course imply money and prices) are *inevitable* under socialism for a long time, but that they constitute a standing danger to the system and unless strictly hedged in and controlled will lead to degeneration and retrogression. In the words of the editorial on Yugoslavia:

We are not suggesting that production for profit can be immediately abolished, still less that a socialist society can hope to dispense with market relations in any near future. But we are saying that production for profit must be systematically discouraged and rapidly reduced to the smallest possible compass, and that market relations must be strictly supervised and controlled lest, like a metastasizing cancer, they get out of hand and fatally undermine the health of the socialist body politic. (p. 588)

Essentially the same point was made by Paul Baran and me in somewhat different terms:

Marx emphasized in his *Critique of the Gotha Program* that the principle of equivalent exchange must survive in a socialist society for a considerable period as a guide to the efficient allocation and utilization of human and material resources. By the same token, however, the evolution of socialism into communism requires an unremitting struggle *against* the principle, with a view to its ultimate replacement by the ideal "from each according to his ability, to each according to his need." . . . This is obviously not to imply that the communist society of the future can dispense with rational calculation; what it does indicate is that the nature of the rationality involved in economic calculation undergoes a profound change. And this change in turn is but one manifestation of a thoroughgoing transformation of human needs and of the relations among men in society. (*Monopoly Capital* [New York: Monthly Review Press, 1966], p. 337n)

And I was at pains to state in the article criticized by Bettelheim that the important thing is not the existence of market relations in the Czech economy or even their present scope as compared to centralized planning; rather, "what is important is . . . the direction in which the system is moving, and here there can be no doubt (a) that the weight of the market elements has been growing for at least the last five years and (b) that one of the purposes of the liberalizing reforms of the last eight months has been to remove obstacles to the further streamlining of the Czech economy along market lines."* (p. 6 above) And again: "The contention is that whoever acts to strengthen the market instead of struggling against the market is, regardless of intentions, promoting capitalism and not socialism." (p. 8 above)

A corollary of this position is that the market/plan contradiction is not an absolute contradiction in the sense that the two forces cannot exist side by side; it is a contradiction in the sense that the two forces are in opposition to each other and are necessarily locked in an uninterrupted struggle for dominance. The question here is not how extensively the market is used, but the degree to which the market is used as an *independent* regulator. And of course this is not in the least a question of economic "laws" or of the consequences of certain economic forms. Rather it is a question of state power and economic policy. I must therefore reject entirely the line of criticism so much stressed by Bettelheim, to the effect that I am concerned only with surface phenomena, economic forms, secondary facts, etc. On the contrary, I am concerned with those ultimate questions which are decisive for the society of transition: the questions of the location of power and its uses to determine whether the society moves forward to socialism or backward to capitalism.

---

* This is of course a very summary statement which does not take account of the possibility of *temporary* and *reversible* moves in one direction or the other. As Lenin saw it, NEP was precisely a move of this kind. But the increasing reliance on the market in the Soviet Union and Eastern Europe today is something entirely different. It is not regarded as a temporary retreat but rather as a socialist advance which receives ideological approval and legitimation.

This leads logically to a consideration of Bettelheim's theory that a new bourgeoisie has come to power in the Soviet Union and the other Eastern European countries and that it is only because of this that market relations have been encouraged and extended in recent years. He clearly believes that the Twentieth Congress marked a turning point in this process, but he also affirms that it "could not have had its particular content or effects if there had not *already* existed social relationships unfavorable to the dictatorship of the proletariat" and adds that this is "a good indication that the development of these social relationships was not 'determined' by the development of the market, but on the contrary was *anterior* to it."

I see the process in question somewhat differently, with the relationship between the development of a new bourgeoisie and the extension of the market being not a simple one of cause and effect but rather a dialectical one of reciprocal interaction. First comes the consolidation of power by a bureaucratic ruling stratum (not yet a ruling *class*), accompanied and followed by the depoliticizing of the masses. Without revolutionary enthusiasm and mass participation, centralized planning becomes increasingly authoritarian and rigid with resulting multiplication of economic difficulties and failures. In an attempt to solve these increasingly serious problems, the rulers turn to capitalist techniques, vesting increasing power within the economic enterprises in managements and relying for their guidance and control less and less on centralized planning and more and more on the impersonal pressures of the market. Under these circumstances the juridical form of state property becomes increasingly empty and real power over the means of production, which is the essence of the ownership concept, gravitates into the hands of the managerial elite. It is this group "owning" the means of production which tends to develop into a new type of bourgeoisie, which naturally favors the further and faster extension of market relations. This process implies an erosion of the power and privileges of the "old" bureaucratic ruling stratum, with the result that conflicts develop between what the capitalist press calls the "liberalizers" (new bourgeoisie) and the "conservatives" (old bureaucrats). The latter, however, have no program to cope with the society's mounting

economic problems and so can do little more than fight rear-
guard actions against the advance of the market- and profit-
oriented new bourgeoisie. The logical end of this process, which
has nowhere yet been reached (and of course may never be
reached), is the establishment and legitimation of new forms of
corporate private property. Only when this has occurred will
we be able to speak of a new ruling class in the full sense of
the term.

In practice Yugoslavia has traveled further along the road
to capitalism than any other country, certainly much further
than the Soviet Union where the old bureaucratic ruling stratum
became extremely powerful and well entrenched in the three
decades of Stalin's rule. It seems to me that the present phase
of development in the Soviet Union can best be interpreted
as one in which the bureaucratic elements, under the leadership
of Brezhnev and Kosygin, are attempting to stem the further
advance of the new managerial elite. For reasons already indicated, I doubt that they can succeed—though ot course they
may slow down or even halt the process for quite a few years.

In my piece on Czechoslovakia I said that there are two
possible responses to the failures of bureaucratic planning, one
being increasing reliance on the market and the other "a cultural revolution in the specific sense that the Chinese have given
to that term: an all-out campaign to rouse the masses, to
elevate the general level of political consciousness, to revitalize
socialist ideals, to give increasing responsibility to the producers
themselves at all levels of decision-making." Bettelheim interprets
this to mean that I believe "the Soviet leaders . . . could have
made a 'choice' between two 'techniques.' " Actually, I used
neither of the two words he puts in quotation marks. I said,
as above, that there are "two possible responses," and I added
that for historical reasons the Soviet leadership was incapable
of making the cultural revolution response. It should therefore
be apparent, I think, that I have no disagreement with Bettelheim when he writes that "what is involved here is not a 'choice'
between two techniques that would enable the economy to 'progress,' but a *line of demarcation* between two political courses.
. . ." But when he adds "between two classes," I am not sure
that I follow his thought.

If he means that one political course (reliance on the market) is in the interests of the new bourgeoisie, and the other (a cultural revolution) is in the interests of the proletariat, I understand and agree. But if—as seems more likely from other passages—he means that which course will be followed depends on which class is in power, then I confess that I do not know what kind of *concrete* phenomena he is referring to. Take the Chinese case, for example. There is little doubt that a bureaucratic ruling stratum was growing and consolidating its power in China during the 1950's and early 1960's. By 1966 it seems clear that it already had a majority in the Central Committee of the Communist Party and occupied most of the decisive posts in the central and regional administrations. Most likely it would have soon moved in the direction of capitalism already pioneered by the Eastern European countries. But Mao and a small group of faithful followers refused to acquiesce in this retrogression. Using the at least partly spontaneous Red Guard movement as their initial weapon, they launched the Cultural Revolution, roused the masses, unseated the bureaucratic leaders, and in this way insured that China would continue on the road to socialism at least for the present and near future.

Would Bettelheim "explain" this process by saying that up to 1966 the proletariat was losing power to a new bourgeoisie but then at the last minute turned around and reasserted its class dominance? If we assume that Mao and his group (including the decisive leadership of the mass media and the Red Army) are "instruments of the proletariat," then the statement becomes a mere truism. But what is the ground for making such an assumption? What do we really know about the role of the proletariat or of Mao's relations to the proletariat? Do such "explanations" add anything to our understanding of what actually happened in the past or is likely to happen in the future? Do they not, on the contrary, tend to convey a vastly oversimplified and hence misleading impression of the relations between social classes and political leadership in the transitional society? My own view, which is certainly subject to alteration in the light of further evidence and study, is that it is precisely in the transitional societies, or at least in a particular phase of the development of the transitional societies, that the "determinist" elements in historical causation are weakest and the "voluntarist" elements most significant.* If this is so, it means that in analyzing these societies we must be specially on guard against thinking in terms of dogmas and formulas.

Bettelheim's interesting remarks on the Cuban situation could easily form the starting point for an extended discussion. I will content myself with two points: (1) I think he greatly exaggerates the extent to which Fidel is under the sway of what Bettelheim calls the myth of the "disappearance" of market relations, money, prices, etc. Fidel knows, and has said on numerous occasions, that it is impossible to abolish overnight these economic categories inherited from capitalism. At the same time I believe Bettelheim is right in implying that serious errors have been made by the Cubans in shaping and implementing their economic policies. (2) I do not believe—and this is essentially a point that has already been made—that it helps to explain the nature of these policies and errors to say that they are "related to political domination by a 'radicalized' section of the petty bourgeoisie." This is a formula, not an explanation. For the rest, my views on the Cuban situation are set forth in considerable detail in Leo Huberman's and my book *Socialism in Cuba*. (New York: Monthly Review Press, 1969)

In closing I want to say that though a discussion of this sort perhaps unavoidably stresses differences of opinion, nevertheless I find myself in far-reaching agreement with Charles Bettelheim's views on the transition economy as expressed in his book *La transition vers l'économie socialiste*. In particular I agree wholeheartedly with his penetrating analysis of property relationships in the transition society. As summed up by his friend Gilles Martinet, Bettelheim's theory

underlines . . . the relativity of the notion of property. Each economic unit is answerable at one and the same time to the state and to its own management. When the planning is overriding and rigorous, the state exercises to the maximum its powers as owner. But when planning becomes indicative and when the autonomy of the management permits an enterprise to make its own invest-

---

* For a discussion of the roles of determinism and voluntarism in Marxist theory, see pp. 79-92 below.

ments, to negotiate contracts, to decide on its production processes, this enterprise tends to substitute for the fiction of state property a new form of collective property.*

I would prefer the term "corporate" to "collective" here since, at least in English, the latter is often used to refer to the whole society. But in substance this expresses in elegant form one of the crucial facets of what I called the plan/market contradiction.

I am hopeful that at long last we may be taking the first steps toward a viable theory of what is surely, along with imperialism, one of the two decisive phenomena of the world scene in the second half of the twentieth century, the society in transition between capitalism and socialism. But at the same time we should recognize that they are only first steps and that we need to know a great deal more about what is happening in the transitional societies. Bettelheim has perhaps done more than any one else to open up a tremendous and exciting field of study.

---

* Gilles Martinet, *La conquête des pouvoirs* (Paris: Editions du Seuil, 1968), p. 95.

More on the Society of Transition

by Charles Bettelheim

Your answer to my letter raises some problems of crucial importance. I believe it should greatly help us to clarify our positions further, and thus to get to the heart of a certain number of questions.

My intention is not to take up all the points raised by your text (as a matter of fact, I am planning to deal with a number of these problems in a forthcoming book).* Therefore, I would like to limit myself to a few thoughts on certain ideas you expressed.

Plan and Market

I have the impression, particularly from reading your footnote on p. 28 above, that we have partially reached agreement on the problem of "plan and market," since you admit, it seems to me, that retrogression or progress, in the course of a given period, of market relations is not sufficient to characterize advance toward or retreat from socialism, and that what is *politically* significant, meaning from a class point of view, is the way in which a possible advance of market relations is handled. The degree of extension, at a given moment, of market relations is not sufficient, therefore, to indicate the degree of advance toward socialism (by this reckoning, moreover, the

---

* The book has now been published: Charles Bettelheim, *Calcul économique et formes de propriété* (Paris: Maspero, 1970).—Ed.

34

Soviet Union would never have been as close to socialism as it was during the period of War Communism).

Fundamentally, the advance toward socialism is nothing other than the increasing domination by the immediate producers over their conditions of existence and therefore, in the first instance, over their means of production and their products. This domination can only be collective, and what is called an "economic plan" is one of the means of this domination, but only in politically determined conditions, for want of which the "plan" is only a particular method used by a dominant class, distinct from the immediate producers living off the product of their own work, in order to assure its own domination over the means of production and over the currently obtained products.

However, your formulations on pp. 28-29 attribute to the "plan/market contradiction" a meaning that to my way of thinking it cannot have. I would like to express briefly my reasons for believing this.

It seems difficult to me to argue that the terms "market" and "plan" correspond to empirical and descriptive ideas and not to theoretically elaborated scientific concepts. These terms therefore refer to forms of representation (*Darstellung*) which they express in ideological terms, and not to real relations. Such relations, in effect, can be brought to light only by what Marx calls an "analysis of forms." It is in this sense that the "plan/market" contradiction remains, in my opinion, a "surface effect," the meaning of which cannot be grasped on the level of this contradiction itself, but only by bringing to light the underlying contradictions (which concern *production relations and class relations*) of which the contradiction "plan/market" is only an expression.

Since this is the situation, it follows that the "plan/market" contradiction is not—cannot be—a fundamental contradiction: it designates neither a class contradiction (a political contradiction) nor an economic contradiction (a contradiction between social relations in effect on the economic level), but certain variable consequences of these contradictions and the "places" where these consequences manifest themselves.

To be more precise, I would say that the "plan/market" contradiction indicates, in a metaphorical way, a contradiction between two "areas of representations," two "stages."*

"Actors"—buyers, sellers, central planners, directors of enterprises, administrators, etc.—intervene, on the descriptive level, on these two "stages." These actors appear there not as *bearers* of social relations and *agents* fulfilling *functions* (determined by the existing social relations and fundamentally by the dominant production relations), but as "subjects" equipped with "autonomy," with a certain "psychology," etc.

The presence of these "actors," the "setting" in which they intervene (the office of planning, the enterprise management, etc.), *the form of the relations* which seem "to tie them together," conceal what is *essential*: *the fundamental social relations of which they are the bearers and which reproduce themselves "elsewhere."* This "elsewhere" means: the economic realm (the places of production), the political realm (the organs of power), the ideological realm (essentially the ideological apparatuses: schools, universities, the press, radio, etc.).

If one exaggerates the importance of these two "stages" ("market" and "plan") to the point of seeing in them the "location" of a fundamental contradiction, one substitutes for concrete analysis of real social relations—generally systematized under "ideological forms"—a description of the "acts" of those who occupy the *forefront of these two stages* and of the *forms* in which real social relations present themselves (*sich darstellen*) on these two "stages."

A large part of the *debates* on the problems of the transition—and a large part of the *policies* that these debates "describe"—has been distorted by the fact that the "market" and the "plan" have been taken for something other than what they are, i.e., the metaphorical designation of the *"places,"* *at one and the same time imaginary and real, where real*

---

* Evidently it is not by accident that revisionism has chosen to develop its "arguments" in favor of "economic reforms" precisely on the "basis" of the "plan/market" contradiction (cf. the book of Ota Sik, *Plan and Market Under Socialism* [Prague: Maison d'Edition de L'Académie des Sciences, 1967], p. 382).

relations "present themselves" in such a way as to lead to their being ignored.

The description of the problems of transition in terms of "plan" and "market" surely permits taking a first look at "what happens" on the two "stages," but it requires having recourse to a series of notions that are precisely those in terms of which the actors on these stages "think" their actions (and ignore the real relations of which they are the bearers). These notions reach back to the multiple forms under which the real relationships both appear and conceal themselves (in the very way in which the value form represents a social relation all the while concealing it). This dissimulation is doubled by a series of displacements, which are made inevitable by the fact that the relations and contradictions which develop in reality (and of which only the indirect and distorted effects are perceived if they were not analyzed as such) are situated on the level of the three fundamental realms of the social structure. This derivation multiplies the real relations which are thus "represented"; it is *indicated* by the "nature" of the forms and of the ideological notions that are introduced into the debates on the "plan" and "market": the value form, prices, contracts, administrative orders, state property, material "incentives," moral "incentives," etc.

This diversity and heterogeneity of notions upon which one is thrown back when one wants to make the "plan/market contradiction" actually "function," really disclose that, far from being a fundamental contradiction, this is only the ideological formalization of the "stages" where forms confront each other which both "express" and "conceal" real social relations. *It is the combination of these relations* which constitutes the fundamental structure within which the *real contradictions* develop, contradictions which it is necessary to bring to light, which can only be done by analyzing the fundamental structure of social formations in transition.

While one remains a prisoner (as we have all remained for so many years) of the forms of immediate representation and of ideological notions built upon them, one is trapped in a world partly real and partly illusory.

"Partly real" because of course the terms "market," "plan," "administrative orders," etc. correspond to certain realities. "Partly imaginary" because the notions which describe these realities also allude to realities other than those they directly refer to, and these other realities remain hidden as long as these allusions are not deciphered. For example, the "plan" is very much a real political and administrative act, but the effective processes of *work, production, distribution, consumption* which take place in the work places, in the production units, in the consumption units, and which the plan is supposed to determine, can only have a very distant relation to what the plan anticipates, a circumstance which can transform the latter into a "mythical reality." Such a process of mythification can itself be analyzed only in terms of class and ideological relations.

It is for these diverse reasons that while one remains confined in the areas of representation of the "plan" and the "market," one cannot elaborate a single scientific concept and can only enunciate empirical approximations.

Such empirical approximations permit, within certain limits, "acting usefully," i.e., permit attainment of the sought-after goal; but these approximations can also lead to results other than the anticipated ones, and that in a way which remains incomprehensible as long as the relations and contradictions that determine the real movement of a socially determined formation remain unanalyzed.

In part, the failures which the socialist countries have experienced have been the result of concepts which have only expressed in ideological terms what immediate appearances suggest.

I emphasize that these failures can be explained in this way only *in part*. If these concepts have gotten the upper hand, it is—in short—for reasons linked to the class struggle and to the relations of strength between the classes.

Thinking about the economic and political history of the countries in a situation of transition, their progress on the road to socialism or their return on the capitalist road, and thinking about the way in which this history has been described and thought of (including by myself) persuades me that it is absolutely necessary to *change ground,* by which I mean that it is necessary to leave the "territory" on which the ideological struggles of the last forty years have taken place. This "territory" is precisely where the "market" and "plan" *stages* are set up.

It is therefore necessary to go *elsewhere* (which is not easy); it is necessary to go beyond the forms which are immediately present and which both characterize the real relations and conceal them. It is these real relations that it is necessary to struggle to *grasp*, because it is only between them that *true contradictions* can develop (including the principal contradiction characteristic of each *phase* of the real history of social formations in transition).

In order to be able *to know* these relations and these contradictions, in order not to be condemned to describe them metaphorically (while believing that one is describing them really), in order to be able to *master* them, it is necessary to proceed to the *analysis of forms,* i.e., to carry out, for the forms specific to the social formations in transition, work analogous to that which Marx carried out for the capitalist mode of production: it is necessary to bring to light the *real social relations* that are revealed and hidden, at the same time, by the *forms of representation* and the elaborated *ideological notions* based on them.

Lacking such an analysis, that one ought to begin to make *today* ("*today*" because real history has "showed" us the illusions which can be built beginning with these forms of *representation*), one will continue to act in an approximate way and, even more serious, one will remain on the *terrain* which is favorable to the class enemy, the *terrain* of ideological illusions which nurtures all forms of exploitation, domination, and enslavement.

In order to return to my point of departure, I will say that to think that the "market/plan contradiction" can be the fundamental contradiction of the period of transition (which I myself used to think) means:

(1) that one remains on the terrain of *forms* and therefore one is constantly led to interpret a *series of effects of real contradictions* as relevant not to these contradictions but to the confrontation of "market" and "plan";

(2) that one is a prisoner of what Lenin called "economism," because a privileged status is given to a "contradiction" which, formally, appears as an *economic* contradiction, and in this way, the essential is forgotten: *the class struggle*;

(3) that one is prevented from *searching for the principal contradiction of each phase,* the analysis of its development and of the displacement of its principal aspect.

It is in this way that one is led to attribute to "market" or "plan" certain "virtues" or intrinsic "properties." In other words one is led to *detach* the possible effects flowing from *market relations* or from *central planning relations* (part of the social relations which ought to be analyzed) from the *political* conditions in which these relations unfold. For *only* these political conditions, i.e., *class relations,* give a real concrete meaning to the development at a given moment of this or that economic form, it being understood that we know that the advance toward socialism requires that *commodity relations* disappear and give way to socialist relations (of which *"planning relations"* constitute only a form, and a form which can correspond to something other than socialist relations: I will come back to this point).

In summary, we need to formulate matters in another way than in terms of "plan" and "market." More precisely, we need to recognize that if "plan" in general is not the "pole" of a principal contradiction the other "pole" of which is "market," it is because the *real contradiction* (the contradiction which the expression "plan/market contradiction" *designates* on the ideological level, both revealing and concealing its existence) concerns the *domination or non-domination by the producers over the conditions and results of their activity.*

It is fundamentally true that the existence of *commodity relations* is an obstacle to the domination by the producers over their products and that the full development of these relations leads to the control over the immediate producers by the bourgeoisie, and therefore to the non-domination by the producers over the conditions of their existence. It is therefore fundamentally true that the elimination of commodity relations figures among the *historical tasks* that the proletariat must accomplish in the course of building socialism. But it is also true that this elimination cannot be an "abolition": it can only be the result of a *struggle* carried out on political, ideological, and economic fronts, for both *ideological* and *political* limits exist to the elimination of market categories and juridical bourgeois relations (the ones that, as you will recall, Marx characterized in his *Critique of the Gotha Program*) as well as *economic* limits linked to the existing state of development of the forces and relations of production (which explains, for example, why in China today market relations, money, and prices have not been eliminated). This is why the task of eliminating market relations is an *historical* task.

However, there is another point here which seems to me to be absolutely essential: the existence of this task and its historical significance must not be allowed to hide the fact that a "plan" and *planning relations can prevent the producers from dominating the conditions and results of their activity.*

This last proposition implies, what has for too long been lost to view, that bourgeois "plans" and "planning" are possible just as *proletarian or socialist plans and planning are possible.*

Bourgeois "planning" has a *partly* mythical character, but it is nonetheless an *instrument* of bourgeois politics.

To identify "plan" with socialism and "market" with capitalism (which is true tendentially) aids the bourgeoisie (and notably the Soviet bourgeoisie) to exercise its domination under cover of a "plan" in the name of which it withdraws all rights of expression from the exploited classes and by the aid of which the exploitation of the masses can be still further increased.

Furthermore, and this point seems to me fundamental, we need to recognize explicitly that *it is only under certain social, political, and ideological conditions that a plan is an instrument of the domination by the producers over the conditions and the results of their activity.* For it to play this role, the plan must be elaborated and set in operation on the basis of the *initiative of the masses,* so that it *concentrates and coordinates* the experiences and the projects of the masses. This coordination, to be real, evidently must assure that technical and general economic requirements as well as overall objective possibilities are taken into account. This is one of the roles of "centralism," but this "taking into account" will be more effective to the extent that the plan is based above all on the initiative of the masses, and its elaboration and application are controlled by them. In this way, the plan becomes a "concentrate" of the will and aspirations of the masses, of their correct ideas.

If a plan is not this "concentrate," it is a bourgeois "plan" and not a socialist plan; it is not the "opposite" of the market; it is the complement of it, or the provisional "substitute."

What precedes has for a very long time been ignored in practice (including by me).* Now, in ignoring this, one loses sight of the fact that socialist relations of production can exist only to the degree that *there is control by the producers over the conditions and products of their work.*

A difficulty to which it is necessary to keep returning derives from the fact that in conditions of highly socialized production, control by the producers over their conditions of existence requires the *development of entirely new social relations,* and that to the extent that these new relations are not developed, the old relations which permit exploitation and class domination continue to reproduce themselves. The establishment of the dictatorship of the proletariat permits the working class, through its vanguard, to impose certain proletarian relations; this is one of the effects of the nationalization** of the

---

* *It required two opposite historical experiences* to bring home this truth (which had been hidden by repetition of theses on the decisive role of so-called *state property* and of the *plan* in the "construction of socialism") which is essential to Marxism. These two experiences are the entrance of the USSR on the capitalist road and the proletarian cultural revolution in China.

As far as my own writings on these questions are concerned, you have rightly noted the dates on which the different texts published in *La transition vers l'économie socialiste* were written and the changes in position which occurred in 1967. These changes are evidently not accidental: in 1967, the development of the proletarian cultural revolution was witnessed by all; and for me personally it was also the year when I took another trip to China and where I was able to grasp little by little the complexity, the scope, and the profound meaning of the cultural revolution.

** Nationalization in the sense of state property, not necessarily of social property.

principal means of production, for this smashes the juridical framework within which the bourgeoisie exercised its control.

However, reproduction of the old bourgeois relations and of the different political and ideological apparatuses signifies that the agents of the reproduction of these relationships, which constitute bourgeois social forces, are still present under the dictatorship of the proletariat and in spite of the nationalization of the means of production.

It is this which makes the dictatorship of the proletariat necessary, for the class struggle goes on. One of the possible results of this struggle is the return to power, under forms which are not readily detectable, of bourgeois social forces. This happens when the representatives of these forces take over the leadership of the state and the ruling party; from that time, the class character of the state, of nationalized property, and of planning is no longer proletarian but bourgeois. In this situation, domination by the producers over their conditions of existence stops altogether and is replaced by the domination of an exploiting class. (After the seizure of power by the proletariat, domination by the producers has to be assured at the outset through the state apparatus, pending the development of new forms which can be realized only as a result of a profound transformation of economic, ideological, and political relations.) On the basis of the old economic, ideological, and political relations, the exploiting class can only be a *bourgeoisie* which now appears as a *state bourgeoisie*. The state bourgeoisie's domination entails, moreover, the development of *specific contradictions* which call for analysis.

Thus, if one recognizes that domination by the producers over their conditions of existence—consequently over the means of production and the products of their work—constitutes the essence of socialist relations of production, one must conclude that advance on the road to socialism requires a transformation of the forms of this domination, so that it becomes more and more complete. This, it seems to me, is the meaning of the proletarian class struggle under the dictatorship of the proletariat. One of the essential moments of this struggle is the revolutionizing of the various economic, ideological, and political apparatuses, because it is through this process that the

elimination of *capitalist* social relations—which those apparatuses tend to reproduce—and their replacement by socialist
social relations can take place.

The foregoing means that what is decisive—from the point
of view of socialism—is not the mode of *"regulation"* of the
economy, but rather the nature of the *class in power.* In still
other terms, the fundamental question is not whether the
"market" or the "plan" (therefore also the "state") controls
the economy but the *nature of the class which holds power.*
If the role of the state in directing the economy is given first
priority, the role of the nature of class power is relegated to
second place, which is to say that the *essential* is left aside.*

That the contradiction described by the couple "plan/
market" or "market/state" has an ideological character appears precisely in the fact that the terms of such a pair only
hint at the real contradictions, while actually designating *relations of a complementary nature.* On the economic level, the
existence of the market (in effect, of *commodity relationships*)
is a *condition of possibility* of bourgeois domination, while on
the political level, the state, as a form of existence of political
power, is also a *condition of possibility* of bourgeois domination.
In this regard, "market" and "state" are not in fundamental
conflict but rather complement each other; the principal role
falls now to the one, now to the other, according to the
nature of the economic, social, and political contradictions of
each moment.

Lenin emphasized that the statist form of the relations
of political domination always implies bourgeois relations, therefore the importance of the Soviet form of power or of the
experience of the Paris Commune, because these forms of
political power gave birth to "states of a new type" in which
bourgeois relations are relegated to the second rank, with the
result that they are no longer completely "states." The bourgeois

---

* One can note in this regard the maneuver by Brezhnev who tries
to conceal the abandonment of the dictatorship of the proletariat in the
USSR, officially proclaimed at the Twenty-second Congress, by asserting
that the dictatorship of the proletariat signifies "state direction of economic construction," which precisely dodges the question of the nature of
class power.

state (i.e., the state par excellence) is in effect the organized exercise of violence by a minority over a majority, while the existence of a proletarian state implies the exercise of violence by a majority over a minority. This involves a radical transformation of the structure and role of the state apparatus, as well as of its relations with the masses. It is precisely this radical transformation that means that a socialist state is no longer completely a state, although it still embodies the relations which permit a bourgeoisie to retake power.*

The essential aspect of the bourgeois state is the *separation* of the state apparatus from the masses; the state apparatus is "above" the masses, it controls them and represses them, whereas the working-class state is no longer completely a state because it is the instrument of the exercise of power by the working masses themselves (herein resides the essence of the Paris Commune, the power of the Soviets, the Revolutionary Committees, etc.).

The power of the workers can obviously take different forms according to the concrete historical conditions, principally according to the relation of class forces. This power can exert itself, notably, by the intermediary of a "vanguard detachment" of the proletariat, i.e., a Marxist-Leninist communist party; such a party exerts proletarian power to the degree that it is effectively a vanguard, a part of the working class which represents the totality of the class and acts in concert with it without aspiring to take the place of the working class; it stops being a vanguard insofar as either it takes the place of the class or ceases to guide the class in order purely and simply to impose its own concepts.

The diversity of concrete forms that the power of the working class can take does not affect its class character as

---

* In the same way the army, which is the principal constituent part of the state apparatus, when it is a proletarian army is no longer completely an army: the internal relations which characterize it are no longer those of a bourgeois army, and the relations with the working masses are also profoundly different; it is concretely in the service of the people, it collaborates in their work, it no longer lives in a parasitic way, etc. The fact that in the Soviet army proletarian relations were never developed to the same degree as in the Peoples Liberation Army in China is evidently not devoid of significance and weight.

long as the *relation between the instruments of power and the masses* is not a relation of domination/repression but a relation of vanguard to masses, permitting the masses to express their views and the leadership to concentrate the correct ideas emanating from the masses. On the other hand, when the instruments of power are *separated* from the masses, when they dominate them and repress them, these instruments cease to be those of a working-class state and become those of a bourgeois state pure and simple. There cannot exist a middle term or a "third way," in particular there cannot exist a "state power of the bureaucracy," because a bureaucracy is always in the service of a dominant class, even when it abuses its administrative privileges.

The preceding remarks lead to the examination of certain other problems that you have rightly raised in your text, in particular the reason why I describe as a "bourgeoisie" the class today in power in the USSR. The question had to be asked. I did not deal with it in my earlier letter, and in this one I answer it only partially. In fact, this question calls for a long analysis. The analysis must be conducted on two levels: a theoretical level which allows the establishing, producing, and developing of concepts with which to operate, and a level of concrete analysis which brings to light how and why such theoretical concepts can (or cannot) serve the understanding of real historical relations and, in case of need, show how to act on these relations by guiding a determined political action —which, in the final analysis, is the goal of theoretical analysis in the domain of historical materialism.*

---

* As I wrote you, I shall try to tackle this task in my next book, while dealing in particular with the concept of a "state bourgeoisie," with the aim of analyzing the specific contradictions linked to this form of bourgeois domination.

A Reply

by Paul M. Sweezy

Bettelheim convinces me that my use of the "plan/market" couple in my earlier contributions to this exchange has been confusing and should be dropped. I had in mind not any particular concrete historical plan but the kind of plan which would characterize an already attained socialist society. But this is really question-begging, and in the meantime there are all sorts of actual plans in various parts of the world which, as Bettelheim rightly says, may complement the market as well as replace it.

The real problem on which I was trying to focus attention can, I believe, be understood not in abstract theoretical terms but only in a quite specific historical setting. All anti-capitalist revolutions that have hitherto taken place—i.e., revolutions which have really taken political power away from the old ruling bourgeoisie—have been faced with an urgent problem of how to run the economy. For reasons which are probably obvious enough, this task could not be entrusted to the automatic forces of the market (Adam Smith's invisible hand, Marx's law of value) but had to be assumed by the state power. A viable market *system* presupposes a whole set of economic and social relations, including a pattern of property ownership, distribution of income, availability and allocation of productive resources, and much more. It is only on this basis that a more or less consistent system of prices can be established and that market forces can do the work of making piecemeal and gradual adjustments to changing conditions while at the same time reproducing and strengthening the existing distribution of wealth and power. A genuine revolution usually comes at a time when the whole socio-economic structure is in a state of disintegration, and the measures taken by the revolution to strengthen itself and weaken its enemies tend to complete the shattering of the old order.

Under these circumstances it would be impossible to rely on a market system even if the new government wanted to and had all sorts of technical and managerial experts at its disposal, which of course it doesn't. The destruction of the old order, the rise to power of new classes and strata necessitate imposition of new social priorities and a drastic overhaul of the whole economic system. This does not mean the elimination or disappearance of markets, still less of money relations. Wages must be paid in money and goods distributed to consumers through existing channels and in ways people are accustomed to. And in the simple-commodity-producing sectors —which in a peasant country like Russia are by far the largest sectors—markets are bound to continue operating in the traditional way though subject to interruptions and breakdowns. But these sectors, no matter how large they are, are essentially passive and reactive. The dynamic sectors—manufacturing, transportation, communications, foreign trade, banking, public services, etc.—are necessarily under the control of the new government which can in no way escape the responsibility for running them. The policies adopted to this end may be improvised and constantly changing; nevertheless, to the extent they are at all coordinated by the central ruling body, they constitute at least the embryo of a plan. And experience has shown in case after case, beginning with the Soviet Union in the 1920s, that these embryo plans have in fact grown into full-fledged, carefully spelled-out plans purporting to direct and control the functioning of the economic system as a whole. Prices, money, and even private markets remain, but these commodity-money relations are increasingly adapted and subjected to the plans developed to achieve the main aims of the new men in power.

The crucial question needing investigation, it seems to me, is this: What determines whether the process of which the elaboration of these plans is an important part leads in the direction of socialism or back toward the re-establishment of a class society dominated once again by a class state? (Here I am prepared to accept, at least as a useful first approximation, Bettelheim's definition of socialism as a society in which the actual producers dominate the conditions and results of their productive activity—though I recognize, as indeed I think he does, that this raises many difficult problems.)

If I understand him correctly, Bettelheim's answer is that it depends on whether the proletariat is in power. If it is, then movement will be in the direction of socialism. If it is not— here Bettelheim does not seem to be very clear about what the alternatives are on the morrow of the revolution—the old exploitative relations will survive and the way will be open for the accession to power of a new state bourgeoisie. In all this he does not seem to attribute a specific or important role to the development of the market elements of the economic whole.

This schema seems to me not so much wrong as simply not very helpful. So far as I can tell, Bettelheim offers no criterion for judging whether or not the proletariat is in power other than the policies pursued by the government and the party. Is it not essential for the theory to have explanatory value that there should be an *independent* method of establishing the identity of the class in power? Or again, what are the modalities and stages in the growth of the new state bourgeoisie? Perhaps most important of all, under what conditions can one expect a victory of the proletariat, and under what conditions a victory of the new state bourgeoisie? I may turn out to be wrong, but at least at this stage of the discussion Bettelheim's approach does not seem to me to hold out much prospect of enlightening answers to these and other crucially important questions.

The reason for this becomes clear when one tries to be more specific about what is meant by the "proletariat" in the kind of underdeveloped countries in which most of the anti-capitalist revolutions of the twentieth century have taken place.

In classical Marxian theory (Marx and Engels and most of their followers in the period before the Russian Revolution), the concept of the proletariat was, of course, quite clear and specific: it referred to the wage workers employed in large-scale capitalist industry who, in the advanced capitalist countries, constituted a majority of the working class and a very substantial proportion of the total population. These workers were assumed to have acquired, as a consequence of the capitalist accumulation process itself, certain specifically proletarian (and anti-bourgeois) attitudes and values: solidarity, cooperativeness, egalitarianism, etc. Historically speaking, the proletarian was seen as a "new man" formed by capitalism and possessing the interest, the will, and the ability to overthrow the system *and* to lead the way in the construction of a new socialist society.* The revolutionary party was made up of simply the most advanced and dedicated, in a word the most proletarian, elements of the class: because of shared attitudes and values it was by its very nature a vanguard whose function was to lead and guide the revolutionary process. Politically, the tasks of the proletariat in power included repressing counter-revolutionaries (members of the old ruling class plus their dupes in other classes) on the one hand and bringing (through education and other means) other oppressed segments of the population (peasants, petty bourgeoisie, lumpenproletariat) up to the proletarian level. Economically, its tasks were to increase productivity, eliminate waste and irrationality, and move as rapidly as possible from a commodity-producing to a fully planned economic system. As these political and economic tasks were fulfilled, there would be a corresponding overall movement of society away from capitalism through socialism toward communism, the latter being characterized by distribution according to need, the elimination of invidious differences between manual and mental labor and between town and country, the complete disappearance of commodity relations, and the withering away of the state.

It may be argued that there never was a proletariat such

---

* The most important document of classical Marxism bearing on this process is Marx's *Critique of the Gotha Program*.

as this schema presupposes and/or that such a proletariat never had a chance to develop in the countries where anti-capitalist revolutions have in fact taken place. I do not accept either argument. I believe that the Russian proletariat as it developed in the quarter century before the First World War fitted the classical Marxian conception very well. True, it was small relative to the population as a whole, but it bulked large in the major cities; and, as 1917 proved, it was able under the confused conditions then existing to seize state power. If the ensuing period had been even halfway peaceful, I see no reason to doubt that this Russian proletariat could have established itself as the ruling class, governing through its vanguard party (or possibly parties) and initiating the transition to socialism more or less in the manner sketched in the theory. Given its minority status, the Russian proletariat certainly would not have had an easy task, and it has to be admitted that it might have failed. But at least it would have had a chance.

What spoiled this chance was the years of civil war and foreign invasion which followed the October Revolution. At the end of these terrible and bloody struggles, in 1921, the Russian proletariat was largely destroyed and dispersed. "The old, self-reliant, and class-conscious labor movement," writes Isaac Deutscher, "with its many institutions and organizations, trade unions, cooperatives, and educational clubs, which used to resound with loud and passionate debate and seethe with political activity—that movement was now an empty shell."* The Bolshevik Party, once a true proletarian vanguard, now found itself lacking any real class base but with responsibility for governing and leading a country with an overwhelming peasant and petty-bourgeois majority. Under the circumstances it is hardly surprising that the necessary preconditions for a transition to socialism did not exist. The Party established a dictatorship which accomplished epic feats of industrialization and preparation for the inevitable onslaught of the im-

---

* *The Prophet Unarmed, Trotsky: 1921-1929* (New York: Oxford University Press, 1959), p. 6. It was one of Deutscher's greatest merits that he clearly saw the nature and significance of this change in the Russian proletariat between 1917 and 1921.

perialist powers, but the price was the proliferation of political and economic bureaucracies which repressed rather than represented the new Soviet working class, and gradually entrenched themselves in power as a new ruling class.

For historical reasons which need not be detailed here, no revolution since the Russian Revolution of 1917 has come anywhere near fitting the classical Marxian schema. In most cases the proletariat, small and weak to begin with, was shattered by repression and war; and all the new ruling parties were strongly influenced, if not all for the same reasons, by Soviet forms and methods. Under these circumstances it seems to me to make little sense to say that the proletariat either was or could have been in power. What emerged in practice, probably inevitably, was a dictatorship proclaiming itself proletarian and socialist but actually drawn from several classes and struggling with the life-and-death tasks of running the economy and maintaining itself in power.

The crucial question, as I see it, is what determines whether a dictatorship of this kind goes forward toward socialism or backward to the restoration of class rule. One obvious factor is the strength, experience, and dedication to socialism of the leadership. But clearly this is not enough. Leaderships do not operate in a vacuum, nor are the populations of all countries equally amenable to being led toward socialism. Each people has, so to speak, an historically formed character which may be more or less compatible with socialist goals (in this respect, for example, the people of the United States, with its purely bourgeois origins, its racist ideology and practice, and its rampant imperialism, are burdened with handicaps of a truly formidable sort). But even more important, it seems to me, is the existence or nonexistence in the population of a sizable element capable of playing the role assigned to the proletariat in classical Marxian theory—an element with essentially proletarian attitudes and values even though it may not be the product of a specifically proletarian experience. The history of the last few decades suggests that the most likely way for such a "substitute proletariat" to arise is through prolonged revolutionary warfare involving masses of people. Here men and women of various classes and strata are brought together under conditions contrasting sharply with their normal ways of life. They learn the value, indeed the necessity for survival, of discipline, organization, solidarity, cooperation, struggle. Culturally, politically, and even technologically they are raised to a new and higher level. They are, in a word, molded into a revolutionary force which has enormous significance not only for the overthrow of the old system but also for the building of the new.

A revolutionary dictatorship which comes to power in an underdeveloped country with the backing of a strong "substitute proletariat" cannot avoid the same problems which faced the Bolsheviks in the 1920s, and in trying to solve these problems it likewise and unavoidably spawns massive political and economic bureaucracies which tend to evolve in the same way as their Soviet counterparts did before them. But now there is a potentially effective counterweight which can provide the basis for a genuine mass struggle against bureaucratic degeneration. If the leadership is clear about the issues and is determined to avoid repeating the Soviet experience, it can mobilize its tried-and-true followers, reach out to the youth who have not yet been corrupted by the temptations of privilege, and deal shattering blows to the bureaucratic structures. In this way barriers to advance along the socialist road can be removed, and proletarian policies in the classical Marxian sense can be adopted and implemented. This, I take it, is very much what has been happening in China, most recently and notably in the period of the Great Proletarian Cultural Revolution.

In my view it is in the context of a struggle between bureaucratic degeneration and socialist advance that the problem of the market in the transition society should be analyzed. As I explained in my earlier reply to Bettelheim (pp. 25-33 above), I never took the position that an early elimination of market relations was feasible or desirable, and I take it from his letter above that we now understand each other on this issue. What I wanted to emphasize was that when the bureaucratically administered economy runs into difficulties (as it certainly must), there are two politically opposite ways in which a solution can be sought. One is to weaken the bureaucracy, politicize the masses, and entrust increasing initiative and responsibility to the workers themselves. This is the road forward to socialist relations of production. The other way is to put increasing reliance on the market, not as a temporary retreat (as was the case with the New Economic Policy under Lenin) but as an ostensible step toward a more efficient "socialist" economy. This is in fact to elevate profit-making to the guiding role in the economic process and to tell the workers to mind their own business, which is to work hard so that they can consume more. It is to recreate the conditions in which commodity fetishism flourishes along with its associated false and alienated consciousness. It is, I submit, the road back to class domination and ultimately the restoration of capitalism.

I would like to conclude by emphasizing that I am in full agreement with Bettelheim when he says:

It is fundamentally true that the existence of *commodity relations* is an obstacle to the domination by the producers over their products and that the full development of these relations leads to the control over the immediate producers by the bourgeoisie, and therefore to the non-domination by the producers over the conditions of their existence. It is therefore fundamentally true that the elimination of commodity relations figures among the *historical tasks* that the proletariat must accomplish in the course of building socialism. (p. 40 above)

I would only add that just because a task is "historical" does not mean that it can ever for a moment be safely neglected.

Dictatorship of the Proletariat, Social Classes, and Proletarian Ideology
by Charles Bettelheim

Paul Sweezy's remarks in the preceding chapter indicate that we have succeeded in reaching agreement on the basic answers to the chief problems raised by our prior correspondence. The fact is thus confirmed that it is possible to overcome initial differences, even on complex problems, provided the participants in the discussion share the Marxist view of history, economics, and politics, and provided the discussion is sufficiently extended.

To be sure, the discussion between Paul Sweezy and myself, which began in October 1968, has raised "new questions"— but these were in fact implicit in the initial divergence of views.

Concerning a Number of Questions

Proceeding from an assumption we share—movement in the direction of socialism presupposes that the proletariat is in power —Paul Sweezy asks:

(a) Whether, in my opinion, the *class nature of state power* depends exclusively on the policies pursued by the government and the party?

(b) Whether, in order for the theory of proletarian state power to have explanatory value, it is not essential that there should be an "independent method" of establishing the identity of the class in power?

To these questions, he adds two others:

(c) What are the modalities and stages in the growth of a new state bourgeoisie?

(d) Under what conditions can one expect a victory of

the proletariat, and under what conditions a victory of the new state bourgeoisie?

It seems to Paul Sweezy that the difficulties raised by these questions are in turn related to the difficulty of specifying what is meant by the "proletariat in the kind of underdeveloped countries in which most of the anti-capitalist revolutions of the twentieth century have taken place." (p. 49 above) Paul Sweezy, in fact, holds that the "classical" theory of Marx and Engels was elaborated in terms of the historic role which the founders of scientific socialism assumed the proletariat in the industrialized countries was bound to play in the revolutionary process. But, he adds, except for the Soviet Union such a proletariat did not exist in the countries where socialist revolutions have taken place. Moreover, even in Russia the proletariat was unable to carry out its task of providing economic and political leadership—it was largely destroyed and dispersed as a result of civil war and foreign invasion.

I do not intend here to discuss the real weight of the working class in the various countries where a socialist revolution has taken place, or the effects on proletarian state power of the civil war in the USSR; on the other hand, I consider it very important to furnish the elements of an answer to the other questions raised above.

To be sure, the importance and vast scope of these questions make it impossible to answer them in the detailed manner they deserve, at least in one article; this would require an entire volume. It is nevertheless possible and useful to provide some brief answers. The propositions set forth by Paul Sweezy in the second part of his remarks, moreover, contribute elements of such answers.

On the Class Nature of Revolutionary State Power

In my opinion, what makes it possible to determine the true class nature of revolutionary state power established through struggle on the part of the masses—of a state power which has expropriated the old owning classes and claims allegiance to the working class—is the *nature of the class interests* served by this power; this requires an examination of the concrete relations between the state power and the laboring masses, and consequently, of the *modes of existence of proletarian state power*.

(a) *The nature of the class interests* served by this power. The analysis must provide an answer, in class terms, to the question: *"Who* is served by the state power?" Does it serve the present and future interests of the direct producers and, above all, of the working class? Does it *help* the workers to effect a revolutionary change in the social relations, which will enable them to gain increasing control over their conditions of existence? Or does it serve the interests of a minority of nonproducers—and this may be the case even if this minority proclaims its "dedication to the cause of socialism"?

(b) The *concrete relations* between the organs of state power and the laboring masses. Today, in the light of historical experience and of theoretical analysis of this experience, it is clear that one can speak of *proletarian state power* only if its *actual practices* reflect specific characteristics, and if the ruling party follows a *proletarian* line.

The Characteristics of Proletarian State Power

In view of long-standing and persisting confusion in this connection, it should be recalled that the essential effect of the dictatorship of the proletariat is to make it possible to establish some of the political conditions that must obtain before the direct producers can achieve collective social control over their means of production and conditions of existence. It should also be recalled that such control is by no means assured by state control of the means of production and by "economic planning." Such control—which can be achieved only through a protracted class struggle—depends primarily, but not exclusively, on whether the producers are in power. We may recall here what Lenin wrote in 1917: "The key question of every revolution is undoubtedly the question of state power. What class holds power decides everything. . . . The question of power cannot be evaded or brushed aside, because it is the key question determining everything in a revolution's development, and in its foreign and domestic policies."*

---

* Lenin, "One of the Fundamental Questions of the Revolution," *Selected Works,* Vol. 2 (Moscow: Progress Publishers, 1967), p. 255.

Control by the workers over their conditions of existence requires above all the dismantling of the old state apparatus and its replacement by a radically different apparatus. A new state apparatus that is essentially *similar* to the old apparatus will of necessity reproduce the *same social relationships*.

The basic *difference* between a proletarian state apparatus and a bourgeois state apparatus is the *non-separation* of the proletarian state apparatus from the masses, its *subordination* to the masses, i.e., the disappearance of what Lenin called "a state in the proper sense,"* and its replacement by "the proletariat organized as the ruling class."**

Control by the direct producers over their conditions of existence presupposes the destruction of the *old kind of state apparatus* which monopolizes all crucial political decisions as well as the means of their implementation, and which has at its disposal autonomous repressive forces which it does not hesitate to use against the laboring masses.

Without resorting to the formalistic use of "abstract criteria" posited without any reference to time and place, it can be stated that an extremely important characteristic of non-proletarian state power, or of state power that has largely ceased to be proletarian, is the fact that the state apparatus is placed above the masses and acts in an authoritarian manner with respect to the masses.

This characteristic of non-proletarian state power becomes even more significant when the *subordination* of the masses to the state apparatus is paralleled by an analogous relationship between the masses and the ruling party. (I will return to this point.)

When the state apparatus exists apart from the masses and stands above them, and the ruling party promotes this situation instead of struggling against it, the objective conditions obtain for the reproduction of political relations of oppression within which relations of exploitation can also be reproduced. Such relations of exploitation obtain when the non-producers

---

* Cf. Lenin's notes on the *Critique of the Gotha Program*, made in January-February 1917.

** Lenin, "The State and Revolution," *Selected Works*, Vol. 2 (Moscow: Progress Publishers, 1967), p. 285.

exact surplus labor from the direct producers, and when the use made of the product of this surplus labor is not determined by the producers themselves; and this applies even if the determining agency is an "economic plan." It is also known that there may be exploitation even if the product of surplus labor is not individually consumed by those who determine the manner in which it is used. In any case, capitalist exploitation is primarily exploitation with a view to accumulation and not consumption.

In brief, if the state apparatus which owns the means of production (as a result of state control) exists *apart* from the masses, and if, moreover, *this apparatus is not subject to control by a party which is linked to the masses, and which helps the masses to struggle to gain control over the use made of the means of production,* we are then faced with relations constituting a structure which reproduces the *separation of the direct producers from their means of production.* If under these conditions the relationship between labor power and means of production is expressed through a *wage relationship,* this means that the relations of production are *capitalist relations,* and that those who occupy leading posts in the central state apparatus and associated apparatuses are, *collectively, a capitalist*—a state—*bourgeoisie.*

As we have already indicated in passing, it would be dogmatic and formalistic to try to advance an abstract criterion of the proletarian character of the state without taking into account concrete historical conditions, and particularly the nature of the relations between the state and the ruling party, the characteristics of this party, and *the direction in which this party's activities tend.* This is why there is surely no "single model" of *non-separation,* i.e., of *unity* between the state apparatus and the masses, but only *concrete forms* corresponding to the historical conditions of the *class struggle.*

Historical examples of such forms of unity are provided by the Paris Commune, by the 1917 Soviets in Russia, and by the various forms of people's power in China. ("Military" forms as well as "civilian" forms: the People's Liberation Army is undoubtedly the first army which is not separate from the people but, on the contrary, *integrated* with the people and subservient to it.)

Historical experience shows that because of the weight of the dominant ideological relationships resulting from centuries of oppression and exploitation and reproducing themselves on the basis of a *social division of labor* which cannot be revolutionized overnight, the political forms which are intended to enable the direct producers to organize themselves as a ruling class tend, if a systematic struggle is not waged against this tendency, spontaneously to transform themselves in the direction of an *"autonomization" of the organs of power,* i.e., of a *new separation between the masses and the state apparatus,* and consequently, of a reconstitution of political relations of oppression and of economic relations of exploitation. During the entire period of transition, therefore, there is a struggle between two roads: the socialist road and the capitalist road.

To say that a transitional social formation follows the socialist road is tantamount to saying that this formation is engaged in a revolutionary process of transformation which enables the laboring masses to gain increasing control over their conditions of existence, i.e., which strengthens their ability to *liberate* themselves. To say that such a formation follows a capitalist road is tantamount to saying that it is engaged in a process which increasingly subjects the laboring masses to the requirements of a process of reproduction which they do not control, and which ultimately, therefore, can only serve the interests of a minority which uses the state apparatus to establish and consolidate the conditions that enable it to become dominant.

The road followed by a social formation is always determined by *class struggle.* The class struggle pits those who struggle for the victory of the socialist road against those who struggle for the victory of the capitalist road. The former consist of the proletariat and of all the popular classes allied with it; the latter consist of the aggregate bourgeois social forces, regardless of whether or not these forces belonged to the old bourgeoisie, or whether or not they are "conscious" of the fact that the success of their political line will result in the defeat of the proletariat. Where the means of production are under state control, the crucial arena in which bourgeois social forces can be constituted or reconstituted consists of the state apparatus itself, and of the upper echelons of the ruling party and of the ideological and economic apparatuses. For the proletariat to be able to maintain its leading role it must constantly maintain the initiative on the ideological and political fronts. This requires that it remain united and closely allied with all the popular classes that also have a stake in socialism. These conditions can be fulfilled only if the proletariat has its own ideological and political apparatus—a Marxist-Leninist party. This gives rise to another set of problems.

The Characteristics of the Ruling Party

The crux of these problems is this: in order to help the proletariat and the popular classes allied with it to advance along the socialist road, it does not suffice for the Marxist-Leninist party which has guided the proletariat in its conquest of power to remain "the same" *in appearance*; its class character must remain unchanged *in reality*: it must remain a proletarian party. For there can be no dictatorship of the proletariat if the ruling party is not the party of the working class.

It is clear that the proletarian character of the party does not depend on *"self-proclamation,"* on the party's own affirmation of its will to "build socialism," on its "determination to remain faithful to Marxism-Leninism" or to a "revolutionary ideal." Its proletarian character can be determined only by a *concrete analysis* that will show whether or not the political and ideological practices of the ruling party are in fact proletarian practices.

Historical experience has made it possible to provide a more adequate characterization of the class nature of the political and ideological practices developed by a ruling party. This experience, illuminated by Marxist theory, makes it clear that the class character of a party's political and ideological practice manifests itself in the structure of its relations with the masses, in its internal relations, and in its relations with the state apparatus.

If the concrete relations between the ruling party and the masses do not correspond to a proletarian practice, and if, within the party itself, discussion and ideological struggle give way to authoritarian relationships, it is then inevitable that the operative theoretical concepts of the party will become increasingly divorced from revolutionary Marxism. There can be no sound theoretical concepts without correct political practice. In order for the Marxist-Leninist principles to which a ruling party is committed to remain alive, and not to "function" as a frozen dogma abstracted from life, the party and its members must reject authoritarian practices, criticize those who engage in such practices, and constantly subject themselves to criticism by the masses.

In brief, a ruling party can be a proletarian party only if it refrains from *imposing orders* on the masses and remains the *instrument* of their initiatives. This is possible only if it submits fully to *criticism on the part of the masses,* if it does not try to *impose* "necessary" tasks upon the masses, if it proceeds from what the masses are prepared to do toward the development of socialist relationships. For the party to be able to assist the masses in this respect, it must be able to ascertain what furthers this development; it is this purpose in particular that Marxist-Leninist theory must serve.

The role of a proletarian party, therefore, is to *help* the masses to achieve *themselves* the tasks that correspond to their *basic interests.* At each stage of the continuous struggle to transform social relationships, the party must guide the masses with a view to their taking, within the objective and subjective limits imposed by time and place, the most far-reaching initiatives they are capable of toward the consolidation and development of proletarian social relationships.

A proletarian party cannot claim to "act in place of" the masses. For the masses must *transform themselves while transforming the objective world,* and they can transform themselves only through *their own experience* of victories and defeats. This is the only way in which the masses can *achieve a collective consciousness, a collective will, and a collective capacity, i.e., their freedom as a class.*

A *proletarian policy*—the only guarantee that the proletariat will stay in power—must therefore see to it that the masses do *by themselves* what they have an objective stake in doing, to the extent to which they are subjectively prepared to do so. Any violation of the consciousness and will of the masses represents a *step back*. And such steps back may cause the proletariat to lose power.

The role of the party, therefore, consists not only in defining sound objectives, but also in grasping what the masses are prepared to do and in leading them forward *without ever resorting to coercion*, and by advancing slogans and directives which the masses can *make their own*, elaborating adequate tactics and strategy, and helping the masses to *organize themselves*.

The requirements of such relations between the party and the popular masses, and of such practices, make it essential that dictatorship, as Mao Tse-tung has written, "not apply within the ranks of the people," and that the popular masses "enjoy freedom of speech, of the press, assembly, association, procession, demonstration, religious belief, and so on."*

To say that dictatorship does not apply within the ranks of the people is also to say that it does not apply within the petty bourgeoisie and especially among the least prosperous layers of the middle peasantry. The proletariat and its party must lead the petty bourgeoisie onto the road to socialism which represents its real interests, but they must not use coercion with regard to the petty bourgeoisie. They must wage an ideological struggle which will make it possible, in Mao Tse-tung's words, to "carry petty bourgeois ideas along in the wake of proletarian ideas."

Such are some of the characteristics of the political and ideological practices of a party which is both a *ruling* party and a *proletarian* party, i.e., of a party which guides the masses but does not issue orders, a party which *centralizes* the initiatives of the masses in order to help them wage *united political struggles*. Such a party is necessary for the exercise of the dictatorship of the proletariat, for it is with the aid of such a party that the proletariat and the popular classes can gain increasing control over their conditions of existence by advancing toward their collective freedom; and this requires their *unity*—a unity which is *not imposed* but freely desired.

---

* Mao Tse-tung, "On the Correct Handling of Contradictions Among the People," in *Four Essays on Philosophy* (Peking: Foreign Languages Press, 1966), p. 84.

The Party and the State Apparatus

It is necessary here to stress the problems raised by the relations between the party and the state apparatus, for the nature of these relations constitutes one of the essential characteristics of the dictatorship of the proletariat which requires that the state apparatus be *subordinated* to the proletarian party. Only when the state apparatus is thus subordinated does it become possible, provided the relations between the party and the masses are correctly linked to struggle against the tendency of the state apparatus to become autonomous, to avoid the capitalist road, and to assure the withering away of the state.

The *dominant apparatus* of proletarian state power, therefore, is the *Marxist-Leninist party* and not the state apparatus. The Marxist-Leninist party is the true instrument of the dictatorship of the proletariat, and the crucial organizational form of a proletariat which has become a ruling class.

The party's decisive role is related to the *dominant place* occupied by the *proletarian ideology* which the party *embodies*; and this role is exercised not only with respect to all the other social apparatuses, but also with respect to the laboring masses whom the party *aids* to transform themselves, i.e., to *appropriate for themselves* a proletarian world view from which the masses are originally partially *separated* by bourgeois ideology. The proletarian party assumes its proper role by carrying the proletarian ideology within the ranks of the masses through the aid it gives them in their struggles, and by itself drawing the lessons from these struggles—by learning from the masses themselves.

The proletarian party is thus the instrument of the *unity* of the masses—a unity with respect to *action* as well as to *ideology*.

The effective dominant role of the workers grows to the extent to which the proletarian ideology becomes their own ideology. It is thus that the conditions are created among the masses themselves for the elimination of all bourgeois social relationships. For a Marxist-Leninist ruling party to be able to play a correct role, it must always accord primacy to the *class struggle*, and make the proletarian ideology the *dominant factor* in this struggle. In the absence of such a party, the objective and subjective relationships cannot be revolutionized, and the restoration of bourgeois domination becomes inevitable.

The dominant role of the party and the ideological and political nature of this role determine the basic place occupied within the party by the *ideological class struggle*, and the necessity for a certain "style of leadership," for a style of leadership which has been correctly characterized as "proletarian." Only such a style of leadership makes it possible to advance along the road to socialism, not through coercion (which never leads to advances along this road), but through ideological and political aid offered to all workers. Under these conditions, it is the workers who advance along the road to socialism, and this is the *only way of advancing* along this road. This is one of the aspects of what the Chinese Communist Party calls a "mass line."

In this connection, it should be added that if the concept of a "mass line" is closely related to the practice of the Chinese Communist Party, the theoretical foundations of this concept can be found in Marx and Lenin. Nevertheless, it is due to the experience of the Chinese Revolution and to the concepts of Mao Tse-tung that it has become possible theoretically to grasp the concept of a *"mass line"* and to understand that it is through the application of a mass line that a ruling party becomes the instrument of proletarian dictatorship and democracy, for the existence of proletarian power is ultimately decided at the level of the relations between the party and the masses.

The Question of an "Independent Method"

It seems to me that it is not possible to rely on a method "independent" of the one I have just discussed in order to determine the proletarian or non-proletarian nature of political power seized in the wake of a revolution. In fact, proletarian state power is exercised at first on an *economic basis which the mere possession of political power does not suffice to overhaul drastically*.

On the morrow of a proletarian revolution, and in spite of "nationalization" and "state control," most of the old social relations continue to exist, for they cannot be directly *"abolished."* These relations cannot be eliminated as a result of "decisions" made at the "top" by a revolutionary state power and immediately implemented. Their elimination results from a *revolutionary process extending over a historical period*, from a process during which all social relationships, and all the participants in this process, are "revolutionized." In particular, control by the producers over their conditions of production and existence requires a growing transformation of the social division of labor, which will bring about a gradual suppression of the distinction between manual and intellectual labor and between the implementation and making of decisions, and the reduction and eventual elimination of the role of technicians placed "above" the workers.

During these transformations, those who perform leadership tasks and "technical" tasks—the political cadres and the technicians—must live among the masses and share their life, subject themselves to their control, and engage in manual labor.

But the radical transformation of the relationships among the workers and between the workers and their means of production, and the total elimination of bourgeois relations of production and of the bourgeois social division of labor, do not result "spontaneously" from the development of the productive forces. Such a transformation can only result from a *protracted class struggle* waged under the dictatorship of the proletariat, from a class struggle developing along a correct road; this requires a class struggle guided by the most advanced form of Marxist-Leninist thought as it is being developed in the light of the Chinese Revolution. Here, too, the decisive role is that of Marxism-Leninism viewed as revolutionary theory and practice, and this is why it is important to elucidate the proletarian character of Marxism-Leninism.

Marxism-Leninism as the Theory of the Proletariat

Marxism-Leninism is the theory of the proletariat because *it is the theoretical expression of the existence of the proletariat in the capitalist mode of production*—Marxism developed by adopting the point of view of the proletariat, the only point of view from which the significance of proletarian struggles can be understood. We should recall here the expression used by Marx when, in analyzing the historical scope of the Paris Commune, he declared that for the bourgeoisie and for those who adopt bourgeois positions the meaning of proletarian class struggles remains a "sphinx," an "enigma."

Marxism and Leninism proceed not only from the proletarian class struggle, but also from an analysis of the *objective contradictions* of the capitalist mode of production, from the elucidation of the *specificity* of the proletariat's position in this mode of production. The proletariat is a producing class entirely deprived of means of production, totally separated from its conditions of existence by the process of capitalist reproduction; it is a class which can liberate itself from capitalist exploitation only by eliminating not only capitalism but also all forms of exploitation of man by man, by thoroughly smashing the prevailing social relationships and replacing them with radically new relationships.

The specificity of the proletariat's position in the capitalist mode of production *forces* it, *if it is to liberate itself,* to develop a radical revolutionary ideology. The liberation of the proletariat from exploitation and oppression, in fact, requires its *ideological radicalization,* its growing commitment to a totally revolutionary ideology *essentially of its own making,* and *different* from the ideology to which the enormous pressures exerted by the bourgeois ideological apparatuses constantly tend to subject it.*

The proletarian ideology *corresponds to the position of the proletariat in the capitalist mode of production*; this ideology is Marxism-Leninism which, precisely, developed and continues to develop on the basis of an analysis of the objective position of the proletariat, on the basis of an awareness of the contradictions within which the proletarian class struggle develops spontaneously, and of the positions adopted spontaneously by the proletariat whenever its own struggles reach a certain level of intensity.

It is in this very precise sense that Marxism-Leninism is the revolutionary theory of the proletariat. It is for this reason that it is capable of permeating the working class with lightning speed whenever the objective contradictions which grip the

---

* The ideology to which the proletariat is thus subjected is obviously not the ideology *of* the proletariat, but the ideology which *weighs upon it,* or, as Rivenc expressed it in his unpublished text on *The Philosophy of Mao Tse-tung,* "ideology within the proletariat."

proletariat reach a certain intensity. This is also why, whenever proletarian struggles reach a certain level of intensity, the proletariat *finds* by itself forms of mass organization which, as Marx and Lenin showed, correspond to the revolutionary role of the proletariat—the Paris Commune, the 1905 and 1917 Soviets, the revolutionary committees which arose in many countries, especially in China during the Cultural Revolution.

At the same time, the nature of the contradictions in which the proletariat is caught up explains why these organizational forms, which may be designated as "spontaneous embodiments of proletarian ideology," are in themselves unstable and precarious, hence the necessity to build a *specifically proletarian ideological and political apparatus,* a Marxist-Leninist party which *embodies* the proletarian ideology. Only such an apparatus makes it possible to *concentrate* the mass initiatives necessitated by the liberation of the dominated classes from all forms of exploitation and oppression, and enables these classes, through the instrumentality of their struggles, to *appropriate for themselves the proletarian ideology* from which bourgeois pressures constantly tend to *separate* them. As was stressed by Marx, it is through revolutionary struggles, and only through such struggles, that the proletariat succeeds in transforming itself ideologically. As he wrote in *The German Ideology*: "This revolution is necessary, therefore, not only because the ruling class cannot be overthrown in any other way, but also because the class overthrowing it can only in a revolution succeed in ridding itself of all the muck of ages and become fitted to found society anew."*

Marxism-Leninism is the revolutionary theory of the proletariat because it draws the *ultimate* conclusions imposed by the analysis, made from the point of view of the exploited and not of the exploiters, of the struggles of the proletariat, and of the proletariat's position in the capitalist mode of production. Marxism-Leninism was thus able to elucidate both the radically revolutionary role of the proletariat and the global historical character of the proletarian revolution, the latter deriving from

---

* *The German Ideology* (New York: International Publishers, 1947), p. 69

the development of the capitalist mode of production as a global system of exploitation and oppression, from which the peoples of the world can liberate themselves only by waging a global struggle.

The Theory of the Proletariat and the Forces of the Revolution

In the light of the preceding discussion, we can now deal with the following crucial point: once Marxism-Leninism *exists* as a revolutionary proletarian theory, and once it exists as a *revolutionary party* which "embodies" this ideology and translates it into practice, *the scope of this theory remains by no means confined to the proletariat alone.*

This is so because the proletarian revolution does not elevate a new exploiting class, but is destined to eliminate every form of exploitation and oppression. As Engels reminds us in his June 26, 1883, preface to the *Communist Manifesto,* the developing proletarian revolution liberates not only the proletariat from exploitation, but also "the entire society from exploitation, oppression and class struggles." This specific character of the proletarian revolution means that if this revolution is made possible by the global existence of the capitalist mode of production and by the existence of the proletariat, *it concerns not only the proletariat,* but also all the exploited, all the oppressed, and all those who are committed to the elimination of exploitation and oppression.

We can now understand why it is quite possible for a proletarian revolution to be victorious even in countries where the working class is numerically weak, and why such a revolution is nonetheless a *proletarian revolution.*

The proletarian character of a revolution, in fact, depends more on the *dominant role* of the proletarian ideology and of the party which embodies this ideology, than on the "numerical" strength of the proletariat. The dominant role of the proletariat in the revolution, therefore, is primarily ideological and political. The proletariat can consequently become the *leading* ideological and political force of the revolution even when it is not the numerically *decisive* force, i.e., when other social classes, such as the poor and middle peasants, are numerically decisive.

We must now deal with an important problem, that of the *determination of the proletariat as a class* during the socialist transition. This problem is related to the dominant role of the proletarian ideology during this transition.

The constitution of the proletariat as a dominant class is the result of an historical process: the process by which the proletariat appropriates its own ideology. This historical process requires the intervention of a specific ideological apparatus, the proletarian party, and is itself the result of a process of *social struggle* for the transformation of society and the world. It is, of course, through such a struggle that the proletariat transforms itself by achieving a unity inspired by its own ideology, by increasingly casting off the alien ideology which weighs upon it, by gaining increasing domination over material and social forces, and by transforming the nature of the productive forces in the light of the *truth* of its ideology—a truth which becomes proletarian *power* as soon as it takes hold of the masses. It is through these transformations that the proletariat becomes a dominant class which no longer dominates other classes but only itself.

The determination of the proletariat as a dominant class due to its appropriation of the proletarian ideology is a process which concerns above all the working class; for the proletarian ideology is precisely that ideology which corresponds to the objective position of the proletariat in the capitalist mode of production.

As soon as the break with this mode of production is initiated, however, the appropriation of the proletarian ideology becomes a process which concerns not only the direct producers, but also—by virtue of the prospect of liberation which the proletarian revolution holds out to the entire society—the agents of other social classes, provided the latter *completely and totally reject* the narrow interests of their class of origin and struggle concretely and effectively for the victory of the proletarian revolution, and provided they are constantly guided by the requirements of the struggle for socialism and by proletarian concepts aiming at the elimination of all obstacles to the control by the direct producers over their conditions of existence, of everything that separates them from their means of production, of everything that divides them.

The ideological determination of the proletariat as a ruling class means that it can incorporate all those who adhere to proletarian class positions, but only if they are fully committed to these positions. Thus in a social formation in transition toward socialism, those who occupy leading posts are bourgeois or proletarian depending on whether or not they are fully committed to proletarian positions. Because this class position, which is not rooted in a class situation circumscribed by the process of production, can be transformed by the ideological class struggle, this struggle assumes overriding importance and may determine the *road* along which the social formation will advance.

It is also because the actual social situation, present or past, the experience of exploitation, of oppression and poverty, facilitate the adherence to a proletarian class position that the poor peasants and the poorest of the middle peasants constitute, alongside the proletariat, the fundamental social base of the dictatorship of the proletariat.

In transitional social formations, of course, other classes and social forces, in addition to the proletariat and the bourgeoisie, continue in effect to exist for a time, notably various popular classes such as the small and middle peasants. In order for proletarian power to be solidly established, it must be based on democratic relations with these popular classes. The very *unity* between the proletariat and the other popular strata (*without this unity the dictatorship of the proletariat is impossible*) requires, therefore, that the proletariat respect the specificity of these strata, so as to *guide* them along the road to socialism, which is also, of course, the *road toward their own liberation. Nothing can be achieved in this connection through coercion*—the use of coercion can only *divide* the popular forces, *isolate* the proletariat, and *lead to its defeat*. This is certainly as true in the industrialized countries as in the underdeveloped countries in which the proletariat is numerically weak.

The scientifically correct term "dictatorship of the proletariat" may have obscured the point that no dictatorship must be *exercised over the various popular classes*. The term "dictatorship of the proletariat" in fact designates a relationship of political domination to be exercised exclusively over the small minority constituted by the bourgeoisie; this term in no way characterizes the relations that must obtain between the proletariat and the popular classes. If at times the latter fall into error, they must be *helped* to correct their mistakes, and not repressed. For these classes are also oppressed and, ultimately, exploited by the bourgeoisie; they are, therefore, destined to revolt against bourgeois social relationships. The proletariat must guide them in this revolt, for *in the contemporary world* this revolt of necessity leads the popular strata, if they are aided politically and ideologically, to adopt the *positions of the proletariat*. This is exactly what happens in the case of the poor and middle peasantry which—if the proletariat maintains correct political, ideological and economic relations with it—will be led to struggle for socialism; in such a struggle, these strata of the peasantry intervene as ideologically and politically *proletarianized* social forces. This is how the Chinese peasant masses entered upon the road to socialism.

In brief, the term "proletarian power" designates the dominant political and ideological role played by the proletariat within a specific social formation. This is, to be sure, the role of the proletariat within each country, but it is also the role of the world proletariat whose struggles have given rise to Marxism-Leninism and to the proletarian revolutionary ideology. It is the theoretical and practical lessons drawn from the struggles of the world proletariat that constitute the content of contemporary Marxism-Leninism. This content becomes a decisive agent of social transformation when it permeates the masses, and when it is embodied in a proletarian party capable of developing it.

Only the leading role of such a party, whose activity and organizational forms incorporate the collective knowledge acquired by the proletariat through its revolutionary struggles, can assure not only the *overthrow of the bourgeoisie,* but also the *preservation of power* by the proletariat.

The Class Struggle Under the Dictatorship of the Proletariat

The existence, at any given time, of a party whose activity and organizational forms incorporate the collective knowledge acquired by the proletariat through its revolutionary struggles does not provide a "definitive" guarantee that the socialist road will not be abandoned. The only "guarantee" of progress along the road to socialism is the real capacity of the ruling party not to become separated from the masses. This capacity must be constantly *renewed*; this also implies the renewal of the party— a continuous effort to avoid the sterile repetition of ready-made formulations, and repeated concrete analyses of every new situation, which is always unique. Such a capacity, in turn, requires that the party of the proletariat *remain in fact* the servant of the laboring masses, that it be capable of drawing the lessons from all their revolutionary initiatives, and that it commit itself to these initiatives and assist in their development.

Unless it fulfills these conditions, no ruling party can long contribute to victories on the road to socialism. If it does not fulfill these conditions, it will not be able to prevent its political line from ceasing to be a proletarian line, and will ultimately not be able to prevent the bourgeoisie from seizing control of the party and transforming it from instrument of the dictatorship of the proletariat into instrument of the dictatorship of the bourgeoisie. The latter, at any rate, may manifest itself, more or less provisionally, under the guise of a "state bourgeoisie." It is, therefore, a grave illusion to view the class struggle as "terminated" when the proletariat has seized power, and the means of production have been brought under state control or collectivized. This is not the end of the class struggle; it merely assumes new *forms*.

What makes it objectively possible and necessary to continue the class struggle under the dictatorship of the proletariat, is not only the existence of what has frequently been called "the remnants of the old exploiting classes," but also—we could even say, above all—the existence, i.e., the reproduction, of the old economic, ideological, and political relations that could not be "abolished" from one day to the next, and that can be *destroyed* and *replaced* by other relations only in the wake of protracted struggles. These old relationships are associated with the bourgeois social division of labor, with the separation between manual labor and intellectual labor, with the separation between leadership tasks and performance tasks, with the characteristic separation in bourgeois science between theoretical knowledge and practical skills, with the *representational forms resulting from these separations* (the *"value" form* is one of these forms), with the ideological forms that are reproduced on this basis, and so forth. These old relationships constitute the *objective base* that enables a minority of non-producers to exploit a majority of producers and make it possible for the proletariat to be defeated. These relationships reproduce themselves over an historical period which continues long after the seizure of power, and this period cannot come to an end until socialism has been *established on a world scale.*

The loss of power by the proletariat is not necessarily the result of a violent physical struggle. Since the revolutionary ideology of the proletariat is an essential element of proletarian power, the ideological class struggle is also an essential element of the struggle for power and for the preservation of this power. This explains why the weakening of the role of proletarian ideology, and the errors thus induced, may create conditions enabling bourgeois social forces to develop, become consolidated, gain influence, and ultimately take over leadership of the party and the state, i.e., regain power.

In the face of this danger, neither forceful repression nor mere verbal and dogmatic "loyalty" to ready-made formulations are adequate. In the face of this danger, it is necessary constantly to elaborate a living proletarian ideology, to help, through an adequate social practice, this ideology to penetrate ever more deeply into the laboring masses, and to help the masses constantly to *revolt* against the old social relationships and against the "values" through which exploitation and oppression are "accepted" by the masses. Only in this way is it possible gradually to destroy the primacy, in class societies, of individual and particular interests, and to create conditions in which proletarian solidarity will be the most important consideration, and the individual will freely desire to place his strength and labor in the service of the construction of a radically new society. None of this can be achieved through coercion and repression. What is required here is revolutionary practice, concrete examples, free discussion—discussion which is not confined to a few leaders but which, on the contrary, extends to the entire party and to all the laboring masses, so that the latter will be led, through persuasion and active example, to adopt increasingly conscious proletarian ideological positions.

Such is the concrete meaning of proletarian ideological class struggle. This struggle bears no resemblance to the repetition of stereotyped formulations, or to the "excommunications" issued in the name of a few principles divorced from reality and practice.

It must be emphasized that such an ideological class struggle cannot be purely "spontaneous," for it must constantly relate to the world revolutionary practice and theory which have assumed the historical form of Marxism-Leninism. This struggle, and the construction of socialism, are impossible if based only on the "spontaneous concepts" of the exploited and oppressed classes. For we know that these concepts were largely *imposed* upon these classes by the old exploiting and ruling classes. Mere revolt against these concepts—however necessary—does not suffice to *replace* them with revolutionary proletarian concepts. It is this fact which makes it mandatory that there be, in addition, an organization which embodies these concepts, and which assures their mass diffusion and creative development through class struggles and constant critical analysis of the totality of social practices.

The role of a revolutionary party can never be that of a would-be "infallible guide" or a so-called elite. It is not, and cannot be, a "representative" of the working class and of the popular masses allied with it. Nor can it be a "substitute" for the working class and the popular masses; it can only be the *instrument* of the power of the workers. Its role is to be an organization which "embodies" revolutionary ideology and develops practices conforming to this ideology—an organization which serves the masses and is always prepared to learn from them. Only such an organization can provide a guarantee that the revolutionary theory of the proletariat will not be transformed into dogma but, on the contrary, will remain a weapon capable of defeating all attempts by new privileged strata to regain power. This, it seems to me, is one of the great lessons of the style of leadership of the Chinese Communist Party, and one of the profound meanings of the Cultural Revolution in China.

* * *

Paul Sweezy comments: This brings our correspondence on the subject of the transition to socialism to a close. I agree with Charles Bettelheim that we have made good progress in overcoming our original differences. And I am sure he would agree with me that many vitally important questions remain still to be explored. That will require much more study and understanding of concrete revolutionary experiences than we now have available, and it will require many further discussions in the future.

—Translated by Fred Ehrenfeld

II
Some Lessons
of Recent History

Lessons of Soviet Experience
(November 1967)

Anniversaries are traditionally a time for celebration, and there is indeed much to celebrate on this anniversary of the Revolution which overthrew not only the *ancien régime* but the whole system of capitalism in Russia fifty years ago this month.

Never before had a revolutionary leadership acted with such profound historical insight, with such bold decisiveness, with such a perfect sense of timing. What had seemed to many the empty boast that Marxism was a science of revolution was triumphantly vindicated by Lenin and his fellow Bolsheviks in 1917.

Never before had a working class become the ruling class of a great country, and never had any revolutionary class fought more tenaciously and courageously against as formidable a coalition of domestic and foreign enemies.

Never before had such radical and irreversible changes in the structure of a society been effected in so short a time.

But perhaps most important, never before had a revolution had such repercussions or evoked popular interest and sympathy on a world-wide scale. The American and French Revolutions of the 18th century shook Europe and its overseas offshoots to their foundations but left the rest of the world, by far the largest part of the world in both population and territory, largely untouched. It was precisely this largest part of the world that the October Revolution at long last stirred into motion and pushed onto the long and arduous road of social transformation. Before 1917 Marxism and socialism were essentially European phenomena; after 1917 they rapidly developed into the only universal ideological and political movement the world has ever known.

"I have been over into the future and it works," said Lincoln Steffens after a visit to Russia in 1918. Never were truer or more prophetic words spoken. The October Revolution marked the birth of the historical era of socialism, and for this supreme achievement we celebrate it today as mankind will continue to celebrate it for centuries to come.

But there is more to celebrate too. Historically speaking, fifty years are a very short time; and it could easily have happened that during its first half century socialism might have made little headway or might even have been temporarily crushed in its birthplace by the forces of international counter-revolution. That this did not happen, that instead socialism spread in little more than three decades to vast new areas of the earth, is due in very large part to the unprecedentedly rapid industrialization of the Soviet Union in the late 1920's and the 1930's. If this massive industrialization had not been successfully carried through in time, the Soviet Union would have lacked the economic and military strength to withstand the Nazi onslaught of 1941; and the revival of socialism within the USSR and its spread to other lands might not have occurred for many years. Nearly two decades of forced industrialization and total war cost the people of the USSR more than 20 million lives and untold suffering. But these heavy sacrifices were not in vain, nor were those who made them the only beneficiaries. By timely preparation and heroic struggle, the Soviet Union played the decisive role in smashing the fascist bid for world power and thereby kept the road open for the second great advance of socialism in the period after 1945. For these historic achievements no less than for the October Revolution itself, mankind owes a lasting debt of gratitude to the Soviet Union and its people.

Spokesmen for the Soviet regime both at home and abroad claim yet another achievement which they believe mankind should celebrate on this fiftieth anniversary. The Soviet Union, they say, has not only laid the foundations of socialism through nationalizing the means of production, building up industry, and collectivizing agriculture; it has also gone far toward erecting on these foundations the socialist edifice itself—a society such as Marx and Lenin envisaged, still tainted by its bourgeois origins but steadily improving and already well along the road to the ultimate goal of full communism. If this were true, it certainly should be celebrated, perhaps more enthusiastically than any of the other achievements of the first half century of Soviet existence. For then we should know that, at least in principle, mankind has already solved its most fundamental problems and that what is needed now is only time for the Soviet Union to work the solutions out to their ultimate consequences, and determination and will on the part of the rest of the world to follow the Soviet example.

If only it were true! But, alas, apart from the pronouncements of the ideologists and admirers of the Soviet regime, it is extremely difficult to find supporting evidence; while the accumulation of evidence pointing to a quite different conclusion is as persuasive as it is massive.

The facts indicate that relative to most other countries in the world today, the Soviet Union is a stable society with an enormously powerful state apparatus and an economy capable of reasonably rapid growth for the foreseeable future. It is also a stratified society, with a deep chasm between the ruling stratum of political bureaucrats and economic managers on the one side and the mass of working people on the other, and an impressive spectrum of income and status differentials on both sides of the chasm. The society appears to be effectively depoliticized at all levels, hence *a fortiori* non-revolutionary. In these circumstances the concerns and motivations of individuals and families are naturally focused on private affairs and in particular on individual careers and family consumption levels. Moreover since the economy is able to provide both an abundance of career openings and a steadily expanding supply of consumer goods, these private motivations are effective in shaping the quantity, quality, allocation, and discipline of the labor force. There is probably no capitalist country in the world today, with the possible exception of Japan, in which classical bourgeois mechanisms operate as efficiently to secure the kinds and amounts of work needed to propel the economy forward.

But the prevalence of these mechanisms, and indeed their very success, cannot but have a profound influence on the quality of the society and the "human nature" of its members.

This is part of the ABC of socialist thought and need not be elaborated upon here: suffice it to say that the privatization of economic life leads necessarily to the privatization of social life and the evisceration of political life. Bourgeois values, bourgeois criteria of success, bourgeois modes of behavior are fostered.* Politics becomes a specialty, a branch of the division of labor, like any other career. And of course the other side of the coin is the perpetuation and deepening of that alienation of man from his fellows and hence from himself which many socialists have long felt to be the ultimate evil of bourgeois society.

It may be argued that while these tendencies exist—this, we believe, can be denied only by blind apologists—they are not yet dominant and they are being effectively offset by counter-tendencies. In this connection, it is usual to cite the narrowing of the gap in incomes and living standards between the collective-farm peasantry and the urban proletariat, the leveling-up of the lower end of wage and pension scales, the shortening of the working day, and a general rise in living standards. These developments are supposed to be preparing the way for a transformation of the social consciousness and morality of the Soviet people. As William Pomeroy explained, after an extensive tour around the Soviet Union:

> The Soviet view is that education in communist behavior can go only so far without continually rising living standards. They say they are now "laying the material base for communism," and that the aim is to create the highest living standards in the world and that the "new man" will fully flourish only under conditions of abundance.**

What this argument overlooks is that living standards are not only a matter of quantity but also of quality. With negligible exceptions, all Marxists and socialists recognize the necessity of high and rising living standards to the realization of socialist goals and the transition to communism. But this is the beginning of the problem not the end. It should be obvious by now from the experience of the advanced capitalist countries that higher

---

* On this theme see Hans Blumenfeld's revealing observations on "conspicuous consumption" in the Soviet Union today, "Incentives to Work and the Transition to Communism," *Fifty Years of Soviet Power* (New York: Monthly Review Press, 1967), pp. 71-84.

** *National Guardian*, July 8, 1967.

living standards based on the accumulation of goods for private use—houses, automobiles, appliances, apparel, jewelry, etc.—do not create a "new man"; on the contrary, they tend to bring out the worst in the "old man," stimulating greed and selfishness in the economically more fortunate and envy and hatred in the less fortunate. In these circumstances no amount of "education in communist behavior"—as practiced, shall we say, by the ecclesiastical establishments of Western Christendom—can do more than provide a thin disguise for the ugly reality.

But is any other kind of rising living standards, more compatible with the realization of socialist goals, conceivable? The answer is obviously yes. We may concede that a priority charge on a socialist society's increasing production is to provide leaders and more skilled and/or responsible workers with what they need to do their jobs properly. But beyond that certain principles could be followed: (1) private needs and wants should be satisfied only at a level at which they can be satisfied for all; (2) production of such goods and services should be increased only if and when the increments are large and divisible enough to go around; (3) all other increases in the production of consumer goods should be for collective consumption. As applied to an underdeveloped country, these principles mean that there should be no production of automobiles, household appliances, or other consumer durable goods for private sale and use. The reason is simply that to turn out enough such products to go around would require many years, perhaps even many decades, and if they are distributed privately in the meantime the result can only be to create or aggravate glaring material inequalities. The appropriate socialist policy is therefore to produce these types of goods in forms and quantities best suited to the collective satisfaction of needs: car pools, communal cooking and eating establishments, apartment-house or neighborhood laundries, and so on. Such a policy, it should be emphasized, would mean not only a different *utilization* of goods but also a very different pattern of production. In the case of automobiles in particular, a policy of production for collective needs means a strictly limited production, since for many purposes the automobile is an inefficient and irrational means of transportation. Furthermore, restricting the output of automobiles and concentrating instead on other forms of transportation requires a different pattern of investment in highways, railroads, subways, airports, and so on.

Now, if the Soviets had embarked upon a program of raising living standards in this second, socialist sense, there would be every reason to take seriously the contention that, certain appearances to the contrary notwithstanding, they are indeed "laying the material base for communism." But this is certainly not the case, nor could it be the case as long as Soviet society is geared to and dependent upon a system of private incentives.* These matters are all indissolubly tied together. A depoliticized society *must* rely on private incentives; and for private incentives to work effectively, the structure of production *must* be shaped to turn out the goods and services which give the appropriate concrete meaning to money incomes and demands. The only way out of this seemingly closed circle would be a *re*politicization of Soviet society which would permit a move away from private incentives and hence also a different structure of production and a different composition and distribution of additions to the social product. But repoliticization would also mean much else, including in particular a radical change in the present leadership and its methods of governing—at least a "cultural revolution," if not something even more drastic. This means that short of a major upheaval, which does not seem likely in the foreseeable future, the present course is set for a long time to come. And since, as we have already indicated, this course has little to do with "laying the material base for communism," we have to ask in what direction it is leading.

The answer, we believe, is that it is leading to a hardening of material inequalities in Soviet society. The process by which

---

* The debate over incentives is usually couched in terms of "material" vs. "moral." But this is not really accurate, since in both cases material gains are envisaged: the opposition lies rather in the composition of the gains and the way they are distributed. Hence it may be more helpful to speak of "private" vs. "collective" incentives. At the same time it should be recognized that there *is* a moral element in the collective incentive system: behavior directed toward improving the lot of everyone (including oneself) is certainly more moral, and presupposes a higher level of social consciousness, than behavior directed toward immediate private gain.

this is occurring can be seen most clearly in the area of consumer durable goods. For most of Soviet history, the need to concentrate on heavy industry and war production, and to devote most of consumer goods production to meeting the elementary requirements of the mass of the population, precluded the possibility of developing industries catering to the latent demand of the higher-income strata for consumer durables. In respect to this aspect of the standard of living, which bulks so large in the advanced capitalist countries, there was therefore a sort of enforced equality in the Soviet Union. In the last few years, however, this situation has been changing. Now at last the production of refrigerators, washing machines, automobiles, etc. on an increasing scale has become feasible, and the Soviet government is moving vigorously to develop this sector of the economy. And while a considerable proportion of the output, especially in the case of the automobile industry, will have to be devoted to official and public uses for years to come, nevertheless it is clear that the basic policy is to channel a larger and larger share of consumer durable production into the private market. Some idea of what this portends is conveyed by Harrison Salisbury in an article entitled "A Balance Sheet of 50 Years of Soviet Rule" in the *New York Times* of October 2, 1967:

In the 50th year of Bolshevik power the Soviet Union stands on the edge of the automobile age that the United States entered in the 1920's. With new production facilities being constructed by Fiat, Renault, and others, the Soviet Union will be turning out 1,500,000 passenger cars a year in the early 1970's, more than five times the present output. But this will not be soon enough to cut off the wave of popular grumbling.

"When I see that any ordinary worker in Italy or France has a car," said a writer just back from one of his frequent trips to Western Europe, "I wonder what we have been doing in the last 50 years. Of course, there has been progress. But it's not fast enough."

The Soviet Union's entry into the automobile age is not going to be easy. The Russian writer owns a car, a 10-year-old Pobeda. He has to keep it on the street all winter in temperatures of 30 below zero. No garages are available. None are provided in the new apartments or office buildings. Most Moscow car owners drain their radiators every night in winter and fill them in the morning with boiling water to get started. There are three gasoline stations in Moscow selling high-test gasoline. Today there are perhaps 100,000 private cars in Moscow. What will happen when there are a million?

Part of the answer of course is that along with the increase in production of cars, the Soviet Union will have to embark on a vast expansion in the provision of all the facilities required by an automobilized society: highways, garages, service stations, parking lots, motels, and all the rest. And in sum, if American experience is a reliable indicator, these complements to the automobile will absorb an even larger part of the Soviet economy's labor power and material resources than production of the vehicles themselves.

Two points need to be specially emphasized. First, even assuming a continued rapid increase in automobile production, it will be many, many years before more than a small minority of the Soviet population can hope to join the ranks of car owners. During this period, the automobile will add a new dimension to the structure of material inequality in Soviet society, which will by no means be limited to the simple possession of cars. Those who have their own private means of mobility tend to develop a distinctive style of life. The automobile increasingly dominates their use of leisure time (after work hours, weekends, vacations) and thus indirectly generates a whole new set of needs, ranging from country houses for those who can afford them through camping equipment to all kinds of sporting goods.

Second, and this is a point which is generally neglected but which in our view is of crucial importance, the allocation of vast quantities of human and material resources to the production of private consumer durable goods and their complementary facilities means neglecting or holding back the development of other sectors of the economy and society. Or to put the matter more bluntly: A society which decides to go in for private consumer durables in a big way at the same time decides *not* to make the raising of mass living standards its number one priority.* And these are indeed the decisions which the Soviet lead-

---

* With this in mind, we can see how absurd it is to describe the debate between Soviet spokesmen and their critics in the socialist camp as being between those who want the Soviet people to have "the good things of life" and those who would impose on them an artificial austerity.

ership has taken and is in the process of vigorously implementing.

To sum up: The course on which the Soviet Union has embarked implies a long period of *increased* material inequality during which productive resources are, directly and indirectly, channeled into satisfying the wants of a privileged minority and mass living standards are raised less rapidly and less fully than would otherwise be possible.

We shall perhaps be told that even if the period in question is of necessity long, it is in principle transitional and will eventually lead, via a process of leveling-up, to a situation in which everyone is a full participant in a society of consumer-durable-goods abundance—or, in other words (since the automobile is by far the dominant consumer durable), to a fully automobilized society. It is a strange conception of socialism, this gadget utopia; but, fortunately or unfortunately, it does not seem very likely to be realized. For if anything is well established on the basis of long and varied historical experience, it is that a ruling stratum which is firmly rooted in power and has accustomed itself to the enjoyment of privileges and emoluments finds ways to preserve and protect its vested interests against mass invasion from below. There already exists such a ruling stratum in the Soviet Union, and the course now being followed guarantees that its privileged position will be enhanced and strengthened for a long time to come. If anyone thinks this stratum is going to renounce its position unless obliged to do so by *force majeure,* he is either a dreamer or a believer in miracles. "Laying the material base for communism" seems to be a slogan of the same kind as those even more famous slogans of the 18th-century bourgeois revolutions—"life, liberty, and the pursuit of happiness" and "liberté, egalité, fraternité"—designed to rally the support of those who look forward to a better future but increasingly divorced from economic and social reality.

The reader will note that we have been careful to speak of a ruling "stratum" rather than a ruling "class." The difference

---

The truth is that it is between those who want a small minority to have the lion's share of the good things and those who think these good things ought to be produced and distributed in forms accessible to the broad masses.

is that the members of a stratum can stem from diverse social origins, while the great majority (though not all) of the members of a class are born into it. A new class usually begins as a stratum and only hardens into a class after several generations during which privileges become increasingly hereditary and barriers are erected to upward mobility. Historically, property systems have been the most common institutional arrangement for ensuring the inheritability of privilege and blocking the upward movement of the unprivileged. But other devices such as caste and hereditary nobility have also served these purposes.

To what extent, if at all, the Soviet system of stratification has developed into a true class system we do not pretend to know. Fifty years—about two generations by usual calculations—is in any case too short a time for the crystalization of such a profound social change. At the present time, therefore, one can only say that conditions favoring the development of a class system exist and that in the absence of effective counter-forces, we must assume that these conditions will bear their natural fruit. And by effective counter-forces we do not mean ideological doctrines or statements of good intentions but organized political struggle. Unless or until signs of such struggle appear, one can only conclude that Soviet stratification will in due course be transformed into a new class system.

That all this is a far cry from the Marxian vision of the future (even the relatively near-term post-revolutionary future) as expressed for example in Marx's *Critique of the Gotha Program* or Lenin's *State and Revolution,* needs no demonstration. This divergence between theory and practice will naturally be interpreted by bourgeois critics as (yet another) proof of the failure of Marxism and as (further) evidence that "you can't change human nature." What is the Marxian answer to these critics? Did it have to happen that way in the Soviet Union? Or might events have taken a different course there? These are by no means mere "academic" questions (i.e. questions the answers to which have no practical significance). If what has happened in the Soviet Union had to happen, the chances that other socialist countries, present and future, will be able to escape the same fate would, at the very least, have to be rated low. If on the other hand events might have taken a different course in the Soviet Union, then other socialist countries, learning from Soviet experience, can still hope to prove that Marx and Lenin were right after all and that in entering the era of socialism mankind has at last found the key to a new and qualitatively better future.

What is at issue here is really the age-old question of historical determinism. The determinist position holds essentially that the conditions which exist at any given time uniquely determine what will happen next. This does not necessarily mean that every individual's thoughts and actions are uniquely determined, but only that in the given circumstances only one combination of thoughts and actions can be effectively put into practice. Individuals can choose but societies cannot. At the other extreme, what is often called the voluntarist position holds that anything can happen depending on the will and determination of key individuals or groups.

Marxism is neither determinist nor voluntarist; or, if you prefer, it is both determinist and voluntarist. "Men make their own history," wrote Marx in the second paragraph of the *Eighteenth Brumaire of Louis Bonaparte,* "but they do not make it just as they please; they do not make it under circumstances chosen by themselves, but under circumstances directly encountered, given and transmitted from the past." In other words, at any given time the range of possibilities is determined by what has gone before (determinism), but within this range genuine choices are possible (voluntarism). This very general principle, however, by no means exhausts the Marxian position. Even more important from our present point of view is the idea, which is of the very essence of Marxism as a revolutionary doctrine, that in the life of societies there are long periods of relative stability during which a given social order unfolds and finally reaches the end of its potentialities, and that these are followed by periods of revolutionary transition to a new social order. This theme is of course familiar to all students of Marxism, especially from the famous Preface to the *Critique of Political Economy.* What does not seem to have been widely recognized is the clear implication that the ratio of determinism to voluntarism in historical explanation necessarily varies greatly from one period to another. Once a social order is firmly established and its "law of motion" is in full operation, power naturally gravitates into the hands of those who understand the system's requirements and are willing and able to act as its agents and beneficiaries. In these circumstances, there is little that individuals or groups can do to change the course of history: for the time being a strictly deterministic doctrine seems to be fully vindicated. But when the inherent contradictions of the system have had time to mature and the objective conditions for a revolutionary transformation have come into existence, then the situation changes radically. The system's law of motion breaks down wholly or in part, class struggles grow in intensity, and crises multiply. Under these circumstances the range of possibilities widens, and groups (especially, in our time, disciplined political parties) and great leaders come into their own as actors on the stage of history. Determinism recedes into the background, and voluntarism seems to take over.

If we apply this dialectic of determinism and voluntarism to the interpretation of Soviet history, two conclusions stand out very clearly: First, the early years—from 1917 until the late 20's when the country had irrevocably committed itself to forced industrialization and collectivization of agriculture—were a "voluntarist" period during which the Bolshevik Party and its leaders, meaning primarily Lenin and Stalin, played a decisive role in shaping the course of events. There were of course definite limits to what could have been done after the Bolsheviks came to power, but they were wide enough to encompass the course which was actually followed under Stalin at one extreme, and at the other extreme a course (certainly feasible and actually advocated by Bukharin and others in the Bolshevik leadership) of "socialist laissez faire" which would have involved surrender to the kulak-dominated market economy and most likely a relatively rapid restoration of capitalism.

The second conclusion which stands out is that in recent years—at least since the 20th Party Congress and the beginning of de-Stalinization—the Soviet Union has entered a "determinist" period in which the Party and its leaders are hardly more than cogs in a great machine which is running, sometimes smoothly and sometimes bumpily, along a more or less clearly prescribed course, some of the main aspects of which have been analyzed above.

Now it is clear that the kind of machine which came into being to dominate the "determinist" period was formed in the "voluntarist" period by the conscious decisions and acts of the Party leadership, for the most part after Stalin took over. This is not to imply that Stalin had a blueprint of the kind of society he wanted to create and shaped his policies accordingly, though considerations of this kind may have played some role. Between 1928 and the end of the Second World War, which was certainly the crucial formative period of present-day Soviet society, Stalin was probably mainly motivated by fear of external attack and a supposed need, in the face of this danger, to crush all actual or potential internal opposition. In other words, the kind of society being created in the Soviet Union during these years was in a real sense a by-product of policies designed to accomplish other ends. But, from our present point of view, this is not the important point. What is crucial is that these policies were deliberately decided upon and in no sense a mere reflex of an objective situation. They could have been different. The goal they were intended to achieve could have been different, and the combination of means designed to achieve the goal actually chosen or another goal or set of goals could also have been different. And the result today could have been a different society operating with a different internal logic and following a different course of development.

These are not mere armchair speculations. We *know* that different courses were possible in the decisive years after Lenin's death because we know that great struggles and debates racked the Bolshevik Party in that period. Nothing requires us to believe that Stalin's victory was inevitable, or that if the Left or Right Opposition had won out it would necessarily have followed the same course he followed. The options were real, and the Soviet Union is what it is today because some were embraced and others rejected.

This is not the occasion for a review of the arguments over what policies might have been adopted and their probable consequences: that would be an ambitious undertaking indeed. Suffice it to say that our own view is that Stalin was certainly right to make preparations to repel external aggression the number one priority, but that a different choice of means could have produced better results in the short run and much better results in the long run. More equality and fewer privileges to the bureaucracy, more trust and confidence in the masses, greater inner party democracy—these, we believe, could have been the guiding principles of a course which would have ensured the survival of the Soviet Union and pointed it toward, rather than away from, the luminous vision of a communist future.

Fifty years of Soviet history have many lessons to teach. And of these the greatest and most important, we believe, is that revolutionary societies can and must choose and that how they choose will unavoidably have fateful consequences for many years and decades to come.

The Lessons of Poland
(February 1971)

Recent events in Poland cast a revealing light on the situation in that country as it developed under the Gomulka regime, and at the same time raise important questions about the future not only of Poland but also of the other European socialist countries.*

The troubles began with the abrupt announcement on December 13 of a far-reaching revision of the system of consumer prices. Prices of necessities—food, fuel, and clothing—were increased, in some cases sharply; while prices of durable consumer goods—tape recorders, radios, TV sets, washing machines, refrigerators, vacuum cleaners, etc.—were reduced, generally by 15 percent or more. "In general," wrote James Feron from Warsaw, "the idea was to ease some agricultural shortages [by reducing demand] while shifting consumer spending to industrial goods." (*New York Times*, December 14)

This reform of the price system both highlights one of the great advantages of the socialist system of economic planning, and at the same time demonstrates how badly this system can be abused under the control of an irresponsible bureaucracy.

The advantage in question derives from the fact that in a socialist economic system prices are not (or at any rate need not

* The term "socialist" is used here and in what follows (except where the context clearly indicates otherwise) in the sense explained by Deutscher: "We all speak . . . colloquially about the USSR, China, and the associated and disassociated states as 'socialist countries,' and we are entitled to do so as long as we intend merely to oppose their regimes to the capitalist states, to indicate their post-capitalist character, or to refer to the socialist origins and intentions of their governments and policies." Isaac Deutscher, *On Socialist Man* (New York: Merit Publishers, 1967), p. 17.

be) set to maximize the profits of individual enterprises. Under
monopoly capitalism, which is the only kind of capitalism in
existence today, prices *are* set to maximize profits regardless of
the consequences for the system as a whole; and this, together
with capitalism's limitless drive to expand, is what accounts
for the horrors and irrationalities to which the system inevitably
gives rise. Under socialism, on the other hand, prices can be
deliberately managed in the general interest and to promote the
smooth working of the economy as a whole. In these circumstances, price policy becomes a powerful and invaluable tool of
economic planning. "It is indeed paradoxical," wrote the late
Michal Kalecki, Poland's greatest economist, "that, while the
apologists of capitalism usually consider the 'price mechanism'
to be the great advantage of the capitalist system, price flexibility proves to be a characteristic feature of the socialist economy."* This has once again been demonstrated by the latest
events in Poland.

Powerful tools, however, can be dangerous as well as useful,
and this has also been demonstrated by what happened in
Poland in December. Poland is run by the Communist Party,
which proclaims itself to be a party of the working class dedicated to strengthening socialism and building communism. And
yet it is crystal clear that a price reform which raises the prices
of necessities and lowers the prices of conveniences and what
can even be considered luxuries in a poor country like Poland,
that such a price reform imposes the greatest sacrifices on workers and other low-income groups (e.g., those who are too old or
too young to work) in the cities, and adds to the already
privileged position of urban bureaucrats, professionals, intellectuals, etc. Perhaps the main beneficiaries are the farmers
who grow much of their own food and will now be able to
expand their purchases of durable consumer goods. If it were
within the power of a capitalist government to impose such a
price reform (which of course it isn't), a law to carry it out
would immediately and rightly be denounced as the grossest
form of class legislation. Does the fact that Poland calls itself
socialist and is ruled by a Communist Party make it any less so?

---

* *Theory of Economic Dynamics* (New York: Monthly Review Press,
1968), p. 63.

No wonder the whole affair was prepared in secret and announced as an accomplished fact without in any way consulting the people most directly affected. The Gomulka regime was obviously hoping to be able to put over a fast one and get away with it. The fact that it badly miscalculated was a reflection of its own isolation from the masses and an indicator of the profound need for political change in Poland. But before we come to that, it is worth noting that the underlying policy expressed in the price reform—imposing the greatest sacrifices on the workers—is quite consistent with the course which not only Poland but at least two of the other Eastern European countries (Czechoslovakia and the German Democratic Republic) have pursued since the Second World War. In his authoritative study of industrialization in these three countries, Alfred Zauberman found that the brunt of forced saving—in other words, socialist accumulation—was borne by the industrial workers rather than by the peasantry (as had been the case at a comparable stage of development in the USSR).* This was pointed out to us by Professor Lynn Turgeon who spent several months in 1970 studying the same area at first hand. Professor Turgeon concluded that the farmers have been among the chief beneficiaries of the new system in Northeastern Europe, and that their economic position there is somewhat analogous to that of capitalist farmers in a wartime seller's market. He was particularly impressed with a great improvement in rural housing which he observed all over the region.

The announcement of the price reform triggered large-scale demonstrations in the Baltic port cities, especially Gdansk, Gdynia, and Szczecin (most likely in cities in other parts of the country as well, but fewness of foreign correspondents and censorship of local means of communication have so far kept outsiders, and probably most Poles too, in the dark about what happened in the country as a whole). The first reaction of the regime was exactly what one would expect from leaders brought up in the orthodox Communist tradition. The logic is all too familiar: the Party represents the interests of the working class, hence anyone criticizing or opposing Party policies must be an

---

* *Industrial Progress in Poland, Czechoslovakia, and East Germany, 1937-1962* (London: Oxford University Press, 1964).

enemy of the working class. Accordingly, blame for the demonstrations was automatically attributed to hooligans, troublemakers, criminal elements, etc.; and the forces of repression (police and army) were turned loose on the demonstrators. Estimates of casualties vary widely, but they were certainly counted in the scores and maybe in the hundreds (according to one Swedish account, reported in the *New York Times*, the death toll in Gdansk alone was 300).

A very different picture of what happened emerges from the reports of newsmen who either were themselves eyewitnesses or were able to interview those who were. And what confirms the general accuracy of these reports is that after Gomulka's ouster (to which we shall return presently), the government itself began to sing an entirely different tune. The actual course of events seems to have been somewhat as follows: The trouble began with shipyard workers who held meetings in their places of work and then proceeded to Communist Party headquarters with what we may surmise were mixed motives— some to demand explanations, some to protest, some to vent long-pent-up anger. Being met with repression rather than attempts at explanation, they attacked and in some cases destroyed Party buildings, police stations, and other symbols of authority. Large crowds were involved—one report from Szczecin estimates 10,000 people—and the army was called in to restore order. The same report from Szczecin tells of factories being occupied for several days "until a truce was arranged: a return to work against the removal of the tanks and a promise of no reprisals against the workers." (*New York Times*, December 30)

Back in Stalin's time a Communist government confronted with such a situation would have reacted with mass arrests, show trials, executions, imprisonments, and deportations to labor camps. The status quo ante would have been brutally restored and enforced. But Poland left that period at least as long ago as 1956, the year of Khrushchev's famous attack on Stalin and of the first wave of liberalization in the Eastern European satellite countries. That was also the year of the Poznan riot in Poland, an occurrence which bore a striking resemblance, only on a smaller scale, to the events of this last December. In both cases the triggering factor was economic discontent; in both cases the government in power began by laying the blame on hostile elements; and in both cases this explanation was soon dropped. A recent writer on the earlier period, noting that at the time of the Poznan riot the official line was that it was an imperialist plot, proceeded as follows:

But after a few days of reflection . . . Ochab [then head of the Party] admitted that riots were *not* an imperialist plot and that recently published figures claiming to show how the standard of living had risen were imaginary. From then on the official Polish line was that the rioters were largely justified in taking the action they did. Later he even had the humility to lay part of the blame on himself and his comrades: "It is a fact that our leadership was unable to protect the country from the tragedy of Poznan, that we were all astounded when the tragedy took place. This means that our awareness of the actual situation, of actual moods in the country, was insufficient and superficial."*

In one respect, however, and despite many statements to the contrary in the media during the last few weeks, what happened in 1970 did not resemble what happened in 1956. The Poznan riot did not result in a change in Party leadership or government. It makes a nice journalistic story to say that Gomulka went out the same way he came in, in the wake of working-class demonstrations. But it isn't true. The Poznan riot took place on June 28, 1956, and Gomulka returned to power, after nearly a decade in the political wilderness, on October 19, nearly four months later. Further, as is well known, the crisis which brought him back to the leadership of Party and nation was precipitated not by the Poznan riot but by a threat of Soviet military intervention such as actually materialized in Hungary two weeks later. Still, what Gomulka had to say about Poznan in his first major speech after returning to power is well worth remembering today:

Recently the working class gave a painful lesson to the Party leadership and government. The workers of Poznan made use of the strike weapon and came out into the street to demonstrate on that black Thursday in June, calling out in a loud voice, "Enough! We cannot go on like this! Turn aside from the false road!" . . . The workers of Poznan were not protesting against People's Poland,

---

* Nicholas Bethell, *Gomulka: His Poland, His Communism* (New York: Holt, Rinehart and Winston, 1969), pp. 208-209.

against socialism, when they came out into their city streets. They were protesting against the evil that has become so widespread in our social system and which touched them so painfully, against distortions of the basic rules of socialism, which is their ideal. . . .

The clumsy attempt to present the painful Poznan tragedy as the work of imperialist agents and *agents provocateurs* was politically very naive.*

What else do the events of last December show if not that this same Gomulka in his fourteen years of undisputed leadership of the Polish Communist Party either forgot the lessons of Poznan or was unwilling or unable to apply them to the governance of the country? That when the workers once again cried out "Enough! We cannot go on like this!" he showed himself to be no more original or no less naive politically than his predecessors.

Gomulka entered office in 1956 enjoying great popularity and prestige. He left in 1970, just one week after the announcement of the price reform, discredited and unlamented. Divisions within the Party leadership had apparently already reached an advanced stage, and Gomulka's once solid support had melted away. Faced with crisis and the evident need to placate the angry workers, the Central Committee acted quickly to dump its long-time chief and to replace him with the man considered most likely to be acceptable to the workers.

That man is Edward Gierek, son of a coal miner and himself originally a miner who lived many years in France and Belgium (where he served as chairman of the Polish section of the Belgian Communist Party after the Second World War). Back in Poland he studied for an engineering degree, rose to the top position in the Party in the Katowice coal-mining area, and was elected to the Politburo in 1959. According to press reports, Gierek managed to get special treatment for the miners in such matters as housing and distribution of consumer goods and in this way built up a considerable base of working-class support. It was presumably this which made him the Party's choice to succeed Gomulka at a time of working-class rebellion.

As always happens in one-party political systems when one leadership replaces another, everyone immediately feels freer

---

* Quoted in *ibid.,* pp. 217-218.

to criticize the conditions which led up to the change and which can now be blamed on the sins of the deposed. It is therefore in such times that we can expect to get some insight into how things work, even if criticisms are often couched in an indirect way. Take, for example, some of the things Gierek, the new leader, said in his December 20th TV speech on assuming the position of First Secretary of the Party:

The iron rule of our economic policy and our policy in general must always take reality into account as well as wide-ranging consultation with the working class and intelligentsia, respect for the principle of collective leadership and democracy in the life of the Party and in the activity of top authorities.
The recent events remind us in a painful way of this basic truth, that the Party must always maintain close links with the working class and the whole nation, that it must not lose a common language with the working people. (*New York Times*, December 21)

One's first reaction to this may be that there is nothing remarkable about it, merely a reiteration of commonplaces that have been current in the socialist movement for generations. And yet, interpreted in context, what Gierek is saying in these few sentences is: (1) that in formulating its policies the government had not been in the habit of taking account of reality; (2) that it had neglected to consult the working class and the intelligentsia; (3) that it had ignored the principle of collective leadership and democracy in the life of the Party; and (4) that it had failed to maintain close links with the working class and did not speak a common language with the working people. Quite some confessions for a Party which defines itself as the vanguard of the proletariat!

Or take the opening sentence of the *New York Times* report on Gierek's New Year's Eve speech to the nation: "Edward Gierek, Poland's new Communist Party leader, pledged today that government policy in 1971 would be honest, direct, clear and understandable to everyone." What else is this but an admission that in the past, government policy has been dishonest, indirect, and incomprehensible to ordinary people?

Revealing as these confessions and admissions are, however, it is important not to be misled into assuming that they reach to the heart of the problem of what is wrong in Poland today. An analogy with our own situation in the United States may help to clarify matters. No accusation has been more frequently or more justifiably leveled against the U.S. government, especially since the Americanization of the Vietnam war in 1965, than that of lying to the people. This has gone so far now that the term "credibility gap"—meaning the gap between the truth and what the government says—has become a household byword. Nixon, like Johnson before him, is continuously and rightly charged, and not only by the Left, with hypocrisy, double-dealing, and deceit. But does anyone imagine that all would be well if only the President would tell the truth about what is going on? If instead of claiming to be for self-determination of the people of South Vietnam he came out and stated that it is U.S. policy to maintain a neocolony in South Vietnam? If instead of claiming that he is withdrawing armed forces from Vietnam he admitted that he intends to perpetuate U.S. armed occupation of South Vietnam?

No, it is not the lying that is at the bottom of the matter but the policies about which a government feels it necessary to lie. The lying only shows that the government knows its policies are unacceptable to the mass of people and hence wishes to hide the truth. The obverse is that a government can tell the truth, and has every reason to want to tell the truth, only when its policies are really those which the mass of the people accept and want. And a corollary is that a government can know its policies are the ones the people want only if it is the wants of the people which shape these policies—in other words, only if the principle "from the masses to the masses" is scrupulously observed. Taking account of the truism that individuals or groups are always fallible, we can carry the reasoning one step further and say that a government can be relied upon to practice "from the masses to the masses" consistently and persistently only if in the last analysis it is controlled by the masses. The surest test of the existence of genuine democracy in a given country is therefore the truthfulness of its government.

With respect to Poland, two things follow: First, by its leaders' own admission it has been the opposite of a democracy. And second, Gierek's promises to give up the old ways of deceit and obscurantism can be carried out only if his government now embarks on a course of honestly respecting and responding to the wants of the Polish masses, the great majority of whom now live in the cities and towns, and most of whom are in or close to the working class.

What do these masses really want? It seems to us that there may be a clue here in the pretty clear evidence that they do *not* want what their rulers have been trying to force down their throats. In this connection, we found extremely illuminating a short piece by Harry Schwartz, the *New York Times*'s expert on the Soviet bloc, which appeared in the paper's Business and Finance section on January 10th. The main headline is "East-Bloc Reform," and the sub-head is "Efforts to Spur Poland's Workers Backfired." Here is the integral text of Harry Schwartz's article:

A cynical Eastern European slogan, "Communism is Better than Working," may be in for a new lease on life as a result of the Polish disturbances that toppled Wladyslaw Gomulka, the Communist Party leader.

Those disturbances were touched off directly by efforts to reform the Polish economy to provide incentives and prods for greater worker productivity. Mr. Gomulka's fall seems likely to discourage other proponents of economic reform in Eastern Europe and the Soviet Union because it demonstrates the serious political consequences that can result.

The economic reforms introduced in the nineteen-sixties differed considerably from one Communist-ruled nation to another. Nevertheless, all aim at obtaining greater market influence on production, bringing prices and wages closer to what is required by supply and demand conditions, and giving industrial and other executives more flexibility and freedom in making managerial decisions than they had under the detailed central economic planning of the past.

Observers have pointed out that the shipyard workers of Gdansk who began the recent disorders were upset at least as much by proposals to change the complex regulations governing their wages as by the higher prices announced for food, fuel, and other essentials. The workers feared that the wage changes would lower their weekly earnings, while the economic reformers were hoping that precisely this fear would induce the Polish workers to increase their efforts and productivity.

Against this background, some observers point out, it is now clear that hostility to such economic reforms is at least as great in the working class of the Soviet-bloc countries involved as among the economic managers who are used to old ways and are reluctant to try new ones.

In effect, much of Eastern Europe and the Soviet Union has operated under a kind of informal social contract understood and honored by all concerned. This contract provided that everyone would be guaranteed a job and at least a minimum subsistence level so long as he showed up for work and seemed to exert himself. It has been a lazy man's delight, a bargain in which many workers have gladly exchanged minimal effort for minimal, but secure, wages.

In much of Eastern Europe, workers who want to do better economically than their factory wage permitted have usually moonlighted. They have worked hard as independent craftsmen, artisans, or builders on their time off, and some have looked at their time in the factory as a rest period in which they could recuperate from the work that was really profitable.

All this has been possible because of the lack of domestic competition in each Soviet-bloc country and because of the egalitarian bias in much of Eastern Europe. The latter feeling has produced social pressure to discourage any worker from being more energetic than average and from earning more pay than average.

But in the nineteen-seventies, the Eastern Europe countries and the Soviet Union are having to face up to the fact that they must meet international competition, and their costs of production and the quality of their goods must be improved so they can be sold in world markets against American, German, British, French, Japanese, and other competition. The spur of this competition was emphasized by Polish officials last month when they tried to win public support for economic reform and price increases.

To Eastern European workers, however, talk of international competition and balance-of-payments problems is almost incomprehensible. Instead the workers see the economic reform and the specific measures associated with it as a means of disturbing the comfortable status quo, while they threaten lower wages for a large number of workers who cannot or will not improve their productivity.·

Given the wide prevalence of egalitarian feeling in the area, many workers view the incentive features of the reform with great suspicion. Why should some workers earn more than others, they ask. Isn't that a return to the dog-eat-dog competition of capitalism, which socialism was supposed to abolish?

In the Soviet Union, the greatest suspicion among the workers of economic reform has arisen from the fear that it would bring unemployment. It is common knowledge in the Soviet bloc that many factories and mines are overstaffed. Hence one way a factory operating under the economic reform can improve its profits is to dismiss its surplus workers.

Soviet propagandists have tried to reassure workers that dismissal of surplus workers did not mean unemployment because, supposedly, there were many unfilled jobs that the newly dismissed workers could take. But the fear that economic reform can lead to unemployment persists. Many workers are aware that such unfilled jobs are often in distant places, for example in the Siberian oil fields, where they do not want to go.

Eastern European economic managers have been most successful in solving these problems when they have introduced reforms affecting workers slowly, rather than introducing many major changes at one time without warning as occurred when Polish prices rose sharply earlier last month.

The implications of this analysis are far-reaching indeed. Its basic assumption, the reality of which is evident enough to an informed bourgeois observer like Harry Schwartz, is that there exists a profound split between the "economic managers" (i.e., the ruling bureaucracies) on the one hand and the workers on the other. *The managers operate according to what are essentially capitalist standards.* Their economic thinking and decision-making are directed to the goals of production, productivity, competitiveness in international markets: these are seen as ends, not as means. And the means to these ends are precisely the workers who are to be manipulated by propaganda, incentive schemes, fear of loss of income, dread of unemployment, etc. This not only *resembles* the economic ideology of capitalism, it *is* the economic ideology of capitalism.

The workers react in classical proletarian fashion. Looking upon work as a part of living and not simply as a way to make money, they resent being subjected to all the typical capitalist tricks to make them work harder. They suffer from an "egalitarian bias" and do not want to be pitted against each other in a dog-eat-dog scramble. They prefer a secure lower income to an insecure higher one. They do not want to be uprooted from their familiar environment and human associations to be sent hither and yon in accordance with the dictates of some faraway bureaucrat. They are, in short, proletarians and not upward-striving individualists. The old centrally planned socialist regimes, for all their shortcomings, did give them some of the things they value. They do not propose to give these things up in exchange for a promise of more GNP or foreign currency reserves or any other abstraction which happens to dominate the calculations of economic planners and Party functionaries.

This does not at all mean that East European workers are, as Harry Schwartz seems to imply, lazy, hopelessly conservative, opposed to all progress, etc. What it does mean is that they are not good material on which to build a modernized state capitalist system fit to compete for international markets against advanced monopoly capitalist countries like West Germany, the United States, and Japan. In other words, East European workers have not been imbued with capitalist values and motivations, and they are not in the least interested in helping their upstart bosses to get into the capitalist big league. Given a choice between a "comfortable status quo" and working their heads off for something they find incomprehensible, they unhesitatingly choose the former.

But suppose they were offered a different alternative, the alternative of actively participating in the planning and building of a better society in a sense they *can* comprehend—a society with higher incomes not for some but for all, with more not less security, with expanded opportunities for developing and deepening the human associations they so obviously cherish, with increasing power to control the conditions of their work and the quality of their lives. To put the point in another way, suppose their leaders, instead of slavishly following in the footsteps of the capitalists, were to boldly "put politics in command" and proclaim the goal of a truly proletarian socialist society. Who dares to predict that, given *this* choice, the response of the workers would be rejection and non-cooperation?

The Harry Schwartzes of course will dismiss this as a pipe dream. They say, with no doubts or qualifications, that "in the nineteen-seventies, the Eastern European countries and the Soviet Union are *having* to face up to the *fact* that they *must* meet international competition, that their costs of production and the quality of their goods *must* be improved so they can be sold in world markets against American, German, British, French, Japanese, and other competition." (From above-quoted article, emphasis added.) To this the answer is, flatly and categorically: nonsense. There is no law of nature or economics that says the

Eastern European countries and the Soviet Union have to get into a rat race with the capitalist world. They have the necessary resources, technology, and scientists to choose their own course and to proceed at their own pace. This of course would require the exclusion of technologically more advanced capitalist enterprises from direct participation in their economies, but it would not mean foregoing trade with the capitalist world insofar as such trade might be advantageous for socialist development. As the Soviet economist Preobrazhensky wrote nearly half a century ago: "The pressure of capitalist monopolism can be resisted only by socialist monopolism."* Anyone who doubts the feasibility of this alternative should look to China, which has already embarked on a course of socialist development independent of, but not cut off from, the capitalist world. And as Professor Gurley shows in a remarkable article,** China, far from collapsing into ignominious failure, has set an example to the world which cannot but have a profound and growing influence as time goes by.

But saying that the objective possibility and probably also the mass base for a turn to socialism exist in the Soviet bloc is altogether different from saying that such a development is at all likely in the near future. As the example of Poland illustrates, the bureaucratic regimes in power in that part of the world are not only separated from the working class, they are profoundly opposed to it in the same sense that the bourgeoisie is opposed to the working class in the capitalist countries. During the week of December 13-20, the Polish workers toppled a government leadership, but they did not topple a regime. Faces have changed, and the new government has been forced to make concessions to popular demands the extent and importance of which remain to be seen.*** But there is no indication of any fundamental change. The harshness and arbitrariness of bureaucratic rule may be mitigated, but it remains bureaucratic rule.

* E. Preobrazhensky, *The New Economics* (New York: Oxford University Press, 1965), p. 159.
** "Capitalist and Maoist Economic Development," *Monthly Review*, Vol. 22, No. 9 (February 1971), pp. 15-35.
*** The best assessment we have yet seen is that of Bernard Margueritte in *Le Monde*. See "Poland: Wage Increases and no more Double-Think," *Le Monde Weekly* (in English), January 6, 1971, p. 3.

And even modest hopes for a Polish New Deal must be tempered by recollection of the Gomulka experience. The euphoria of 1956 did not last long, and in the later years of his rule Gomulka, the nationalist and reformer, turned into an eager tool of Soviet hegemony and a tyrant to his own people.

The best that could come of the Polish upheaval of 1970 would be if the workers not only of Poland but of the whole Soviet bloc would draw the lesson that what they need is not a new leadership which *claims* to represent their interests but a new regime which *does in fact* represent their interests because it is under their own control.

The Transition to Socialism

The subject of this talk is so large and one hour is so brief that I must confine myself to a few aspects of what could easily constitute the content of an entire course of lectures. This necessarily means that I will assume much that is neither obvious nor uncontroversial. It may therefore be useful at the outset to make explicit some of these assumptions.

(1) There is no such thing as a general theory of the transition between social systems. This is not because relatively little attention has been paid to the subject—though this is undoubtedly true—but because each transition is a unique historical process which must be analyzed and explained as such.

(2) Nevertheless, a comparative study of transitions can be extremely valuable. In particular the study of past transitions can help us to ask fruitful questions about present and possible future transitions, to recognize similarities and differences, to appreciate the historicity and totality of the process under examination.

(3) Transitions are never simple or brief processes. On the contrary, they typically occupy and even define whole historical epochs. One aspect of their complexity is what may be called multi-directionality: movement in one direction may turn back on itself and resume in a forward direction from a new basis.

This is the text of a lecture given in March and April 1971 in Turin and other Italian cities, at the invitation of the Associazione Culturale Italiana.

In some places the reversal may be prolonged or conceivably even permanent.

(4) Transitions from one social order to another involve the most difficult and profound problems of historical material- ism. "Herr Proudhon does not know," Marx wrote in *The Poverty of Philosophy*, "that all history is but the continuous transformation of human nature." (Marx/Engels, *Werke*, Vol. 4, p. 160) This view can be squared with the principle, as stated in the sixth Thesis on Feuerbach, that "the human essence is no abstraction inherent in each single individual" but "the ensemble of social relations," only if it is possible to relate the transformation of human nature to the transformation of social relations. How this is to be done is also indicated in the *Theses on Feuerbach* (the third):

The materialist doctrine that men are products of circum- stances and upbringing, and that therefore changed men are the product of other circumstances and changed upbringing, forgets that it is men who change circumstances and that the educator must himself be educated. . . . The coincidence of the changing of circumstances and human activity can be conceived and ration- ally understood only as *revolutionizing practice*.

Here, in the concatenation of human nature, social relations, and revolutionizing practice, we reach the heart of the problem of the transition from one social system to another.

*   *   *

Let us begin with a few reflections on the transition from feudalism to capitalism in its decisive European theater. There are, I believe, many unsettled questions in this area relating to such matters as the causes of the decline of feudalism and the origins of capitalism, but they are not my present concern. Whatever positions may be held by different scholars on these questions, it seems to me unlikely that any would disagree that both the decline of feudalism and the beginnings of capitalism can be traced far back into the Middle Ages, that is to say, into a period when there is no doubt that the dominant European mode of production was feudal. In other words, there is no doubt that capitalism made its appearance, not as a theory or an aspiration but as an actual social formation within the confines of feudal society. Oliver Cox has argued very persuasively that Venice in the Middle Ages was already a thoroughly bourgeois city-state, completely oriented toward profit-seeking commerce, with significant capitalist production (e.g., in shipbuilding) and a typically bourgeois political and ideological superstructure. The same can be said with even greater certainty of a considerable number of Italian and Northern European cities in the later feudal period, and of course the discovery of America and the opening up of sea routes to the Far East in the fifteenth and sixteenth centuries generated a burst of activity (including plunder and piracy as well as trade) which by no stretch of the imagination could be called "feudal." There is room for dispute about precisely how and when capitalism finally triumphed, but there can be no contesting the fact that the process involved an ongoing struggle between two actually existing social formations for supremacy, i.e., for state power (monopoly over the means of coercion) and the right to organize society in accordance with their respective interests and ideas. Moreover the process was a prolonged one in which the "new" social formation had ample time to prepare itself, both economically and ideologically, for the role of undisputed dominance.

What does this mean in terms of the transformation of human nature? It means that "bourgeois man" was born and matured in a feudal world. The establishment and expansion of capitalist economic and social relations were practical human activities which gradually molded human beings with appropriate attitudes, motivations, "instincts"—cupidity, means-and-ends rationality, individualism, and so on. For centuries bourgeois man lived alongside feudal man, sometimes in uneasy accommodation, sometimes in mortal combat, but always advancing and reaching out for more power, eventually conquering and even assimilating his ancient rival. When the time finally came for bourgeois man to step forward as the master of his universe, his nature was fully formed and faithfully reflected the newly emergent "ensemble of social relations." In retrospect we can see that in this case the "revolutionizing practice," which in Marx's view is the key to understanding changes in society and hence also changes in human nature, was precisely the centuries-long process of building capitalism within the framework of feudal society.

*   *   *

If we turn now to the subject before us, the first thing we notice is that the transition to socialism does not, and in the nature of the case cannot, take the same course as the transition from feudalism to capitalism. Not that this road has never occurred to anyone, or even that it has never been tried. Quite the contrary. The distinguishing characteristic of pre-Marxian or Utopian socialism was the deliberate selection (though not the conscious copying) of a road to socialism similar to that which had led from feudalism to capitalism. Small socialistic communities were to be, and in many cases actually were, established. These were to be both schools of socialism and bases from which the new society would spread, undermining and eventually overwhelming their capitalist matrix. There were many reasons why this strategy could not work, perhaps chief among them that the small socialist communities—unlike capitalism in the interstices of feudal society—had nothing positive to offer the dominant system and hence from its viewpoint their success would be an unmitigated disaster. Add to this that they had neither the ability nor the desire to compete against capitalism on its own terms and one can see that the obstacles to their survival, let alone development, were so enormous that they were in effect doomed from the outset. Instead of creating a new socialist human nature, they served only to buttress the characteristic bourgeois view that human nature is, after all, unchangeable.

Marx of course shared none of the illusions of the Utopians and, as we have already seen, was fully aware of the complex interrelation of social systems, human action, and social change. (It is worth remembering that both the *Theses on Feuerbach* and *The Poverty of Philosophy,* from which I quoted earlier, were written in the period 1845-1847, i.e., early in Marx's intellectual development; and there is not the slightest reason to believe that he ever changed his mind on these absolutely fundamental questions.) What, then, was his conception of the *modus operandi* of the transition to socialism?

The answer, at least in broad outline, is well known. Socialism itself cannot take root and grow within the confines of capitalist society, as capitalism had done under feudalism. But in Marx's view capitalism has a special, perhaps historically unique, characteristic which not only makes possible but guarantees the existence of a different road to its transformation.

The essence of capitalism is the self-expansion of capital, which takes place through the production and capitalization of surplus value. Production of surplus value in turn is the function of the proletariat, i.e., the class of wage workers who own no means of production and can live only by the sale of their labor power. Since the proletariat produces for capital and not for the satisfaction of its own needs, it follows that capitalism, in Marx's words, "establishes an accumulation of misery corresponding with accumulation of capital." The proletariat is thus both essential to capitalism and its essential victim. As capitalism grows, so does the proletariat; and the very processes of capitalist development prepare the proletariat for its historic role. Hence the concluding sentences of the first section of the *Communist Manifesto*: "What the bourgeoisie therefore produces, above all, are its own grave-diggers. Its fall and the victory of the proletariat are equally inevitable."

This theory of the revolutionary mission of the proletariat is of course central to Marxism and has been endlessly expounded, criticized, and debated. It is not my present purpose, however, to enter this discussion but rather to point out that, considered as a theory of the transition to socialism, it is only half a theory. What it deals with is the overthrow of capitalism; what it omits is the construction of socialism. Does Marxism contain, or imply, a complementary theory of the construction of socialism? If so, what is it? These are the questions to which I should like to address myself next.

* * *

For our purposes we do not need a definition of socialism, nor do we need to compile a catalogue of its characteristics. But we definitely do need to be perfectly clear that Marxism has always conceived of socialism as the negation of capitalism, operating according to radically different laws and principles.

Capitalism treats people as means to the expansion of capital, which is the root of its manifold contradictions and evils. The main point of socialism is to reverse this, to enable people to take over and to arrange not only their productive activity but their whole lives with a view to satisfying their truly human needs. This reversal implies, among other things, the abolition of private property in the means of production and of incomes derived therefrom, a high degree of equality in all things, allocation of resources by plan rather than by the blind forces of the market, the elimination as rapidly as possible of invidious distinctions between manual and mental labor and between city and country, and the ultimate replacement of all money and commodity relations by direct human relations.

Now it is clear that capitalists and those imbued with capitalist attitudes and values would neither want nor be able to build and operate such a society. Their bourgeois human nature would be totally incompatible with the ensemble of social relations of socialist society. An attempt to combine the two would be doomed from the outset: either bourgeois human nature would have to be transformed into socialist human nature, or socialist relations would have to be transformed into bourgeois relations.

Let us recall at this point that this dilemma never arose in the case of the transition to capitalism. Bourgeois relations grew up within the framework of feudal society and molded bourgeois human nature over a period of several centuries. When capitalism finally conquered feudalism, it did so not merely as a revolutionary class but as an entire social order in which the correspondence between human nature and social relations was already fully developed. The element of dissonance represented by the continued existence of feudal remnants was of course there and in some (superstructural) respects was even important, but it posed no serious threat to the functioning of capitalism.

As we have seen, socialist human nature could not emerge through the revolutionizing practice of socialism within the framework of capitalism. Are there other possibilities, and if so what are they?

Not so long ago, I argued, in a discussion with Charles

Bettelheim, that Marxism, at least up to the time of the Russian Revolution, had a clear answer to this question:

> In classical Marxian theory . . . the proletariat . . . referred to the wage workers employed in large-scale capitalist industry who, in the advanced capitalist countries, constituted a majority of the working class and a very substantial proportion of the total population. These workers were assumed to have acquired, as a consequence of the capitalist accumulation process itself, certain specifically proletarian (and anti-bourgeois) attitudes and values: solidarity, cooperativeness, egalitarianism, etc. Historically speaking, the proletarian was seen as a "new man" formed by capitalism and possessing the interest, the will, and the ability to overthrow the system *and* to lead the way in the construction of a new socialist society. (p. 50 above)

I wrote this not after research in the relevant texts but from my general understanding of Marxian theory formed over a period of many years. Subsequently I was challenged to support this interpretation, and I must confess that I was unable to do so. It is easy to cite dozens of passages from the works of Marx and Engels affirming the revolutionary role of the proletariat in the overthrow of capitalism. I have not, however, found any which are specifically addressed to the question of the proletariat's ability or readiness to build a socialist society; and at least some of their formulations, especially those which analyze the effects of the division of labor on the worker, clearly imply a negative evaluation of the proletariat's qualifications. Consider, for example, the following from the famous chapter on "Machinery and Modern Industry," in the first volume of *Capital* (repeated verbatim by Engels in *Anti-Dühring*):

> Modern industry, indeed, compels society, under penalty of death, to replace the detail-worker of today, crippled by life-long repetition of one and the same trivial operation, and thus reduced to the mere fragment of a man, by the fully developed individual, fit for a variety of labors, ready to face any change of production, and to whom the different social functions he performs are but so many modes of giving free scope to his own natural and acquired powers.

As a statement of one of the central aims, I would even

say necessities of socialism, this is magnificent. But when Marx says that modern industry "compels society" to follow the course indicated, he deliberately sidesteps the question of the nature of the revolutionizing practice which will turn a mere fragment of a man into a fully developed individual.

When in doubt about the correct interpretation of Marx, it is a good idea to consult Lenin. What were his ideas on this subject?

Perhaps Lenin's most systematic analysis of the characteristics of the proletariat was in *What Is to Be Done?*, written in 1902. There, as is well known, he argued that "economism" comes naturally to the proletariat: "The history of all countries shows that the working class, exclusively by its own effort, is able to develop only trade union consciousness, i.e., the conviction that it is necessary to combine in unions, fight the employers and strive to compel the government to pass necessary labor legislation, etc." (*Selected Works,* Vol. I, Part 1, pp. 233-234) Socialism, i.e., the conviction that it is necessary to overthrow capitalism and replace it by an entirely different system, was, according to Lenin, introduced into the proletariat by revolutionary intellectuals. It was they who took the initiative in educating the advanced workers to their real interests and organizing them into a revolutionary vanguard party whose functions were both to lead the proletariat in revolutionary struggles and to imbue it with an ever sharper socialist consciousness. The clear implication of this view for the problem which concerns us is that it is not capitalism as such but the revolutionary struggle to overthrow capitalism which creates men with the will and ability to go further and begin the construction of socialism. Revolutionizing practice, in Lenin's view, was nothing more nor less than the practice of revolution.

We are often told, especially by learned opponents of Marxism, that it was precisely in his denial of the spontaneous revolutionary potential of the proletariat that Lenin differed most markedly from Marx and Engels. This is supposed to be the basis of his conception of the nature and role of the vanguard party, which is widely believed to constitute a Leninist deviation without roots in the teachings of the masters.

Certainly there is no doubt that it was Lenin who was

responsible for developing the vanguard party, both in theory and practice, as we know it today. But is there really any inconsistency between the Leninist conception of the party and the ideas of Marx and Engels?

It seems to me that it would be correct to give an affirmative answer to this question only if it could be shown that Marx and Engels believed that the proletariat was capable of developing, exclusively by its own effort (in Lenin's phrase), a revolutionary *and* socialist consciousness. As I indicated earlier, I used to think that this was indeed their view but an effort to prove it convinced me that I was wrong. Not only does one look in vain for specific statements attributing revolutionary socialist spontaneism to the proletariat, but the lifelong practice of the two men would be incomprehensible if they had held such a view of the character of the proletariat. From the Communist League in the 1840s through the First International to Engels's last years when he acted as consultant to socialist parties all over the world, they were tireless in their efforts to do just what Lenin said it was the function of revolutionary intellectuals to do, i.e., introduce a revolutionary socialist consciousness into the proletariat. And it is of course obvious that one of the examples Lenin had in mind when he wrote *What Is to Be Done?* was the founders of scientific socialism. The weight of the evidence, it seems to me, is that in this as in other matters Lenin's ideas and activities were fully consistent with those of Marx and Engels. For them, no less than for him, revolutionizing practice was the practice of revolution.

*   *   *

I would like now to attempt to draw some of the implications of this view for the transition to socialism. Bourgeois human nature, as we have seen, was formed in a centuries-long process of actual capitalist development within the framework of feudal society. When capitalism had grown strong enough to challenge and defeat feudalism, there was no real possibility of a return to feudalism. Bourgeois man was at home only in bourgeois society: there was no conceivable reason for him to reactivate or recreate feudal social relations. (This is not to deny of course that capitalist power could here and there be defeated by feudal power, resulting in local and perhaps even prolonged setbacks to the progress of capitalism. Such occurrences, however, could not arrest the general advance of the new system.) It is altogether different in the case of the transition to socialism. Socialist human nature is not formed within the framework of capitalism but only in the struggle against capitalism. What guarantee is there that this will occur on a sufficient scale and in sufficient depth to make possible the construction of a new socialist society? For we should be under no illusion that the social relations specific to a socialist society could exist in anything but name in the absence of the kind of human material which alone could give them sense and meaning. That Marx himself understood this, even if he did not explore all its implications, is shown by a passage from the *Enthüllungen über den Kommunisten-Prozess zu Köln* in which he distinguishes between the propaganda of his group in the Communist League and that of an opposed minority group:

> While we say to the workers: you have to undergo fifteen, twenty, fifty years of civil wars and popular struggles not only to change the relations but to change yourselves and prepare yourselves for political mastery, they tell them on the contrary, "We must come to power immediately, or we can forget about it." While we make a special point of emphasizing to the German worker the underdeveloped state of the German proletariat, they flatter his national feeling and the craft prejudice of the German artisan, which to be sure is more popular. (*Werke,* Vol. 8, p. 412)

Here Marx puts his finger on the central issue: the proletariat must not only change the relations of society but in the process change itself. And unfortunately more than a century of subsequent history proves all too conclusively that there is as yet no guarantee that this can be successfully accomplished.

As far as the industrially advanced countries are concerned, capitalism proved to have a great deal more expansive and adaptive power than Marx suspected. Under the circumstances, their proletariats succumbed to the economism which Lenin saw as natural to them but believed could be overcome by a conscious revolutionary vanguard. What actually happened was the opposite: the vanguards, whether calling themselves Socialist or Social Democratic or Communist, instead of converting the proletarian masses to revolutionary socialism were themselves transformed into economistic reformers. There are of course those who see in this a temporary aberration and believe that a new revolutionary period has opened in which the proletariat will once again play the role attributed to it in classical Marxist-Leninist theory. (For an able presentation of this argument, see Daniel Singer's recently published work, *Prelude to Revolution*.) I for one fervently hope that they are right, but as for now the most one can say is that the case is unproved.

When we turn to the countries where the old regimes (either capitalist or a feudal-capitalist mixture) have actually been overthrown, we are confronted with two very different experiences which, for obvious reasons, can best be exemplified by the Soviet Union and China respectively.

The October Revolution proved the validity, under conditions existing in Russia in 1917, of the first half of the Marxist-Leninist theory of transition to socialism. The industrial proletariat, though relatively small, was able, under resolute revolutionary leadership, to overthrow the bourgeois regime which had come to power in the February Revolution. But with regard to the second half of the theory—the capacity of the proletariat to lead the way in the construction of socialism—the Russian experience is at best inconclusive. Small to begin with, the Russian proletariat was decimated and dispersed by the four years of bloody civil war, hunger, and chaos which followed the October Revolution. The Bolshevik government, preoccupied with problems of survival and economic recovery, was obliged to rely on the old, obviously profoundly anti-socialist state bureaucracy and to add to its size and power in the ensuing years. Nevertheless, the period from roughly 1922 to 1928 was one of revolutionary ferment—in the arts, education, sexual relations, social science, etc.—which, had it not been cut short, might have generated powerful socialist forces and trends. What brought this period to an end was the fateful decision to subordinate everything else to the most rapid possible economic development. It would take us too far afield to discuss the reasons for or justification of this decision: suffice it to point out that it entailed what may almost be called a cultural counter-revolution together with the imposition of an extremely repressive political regime. Under the circumstances, revolutionizing practice tending to produce socialist human nature almost totally disappeared. Instead, the reconstituted and expanded proletariat which came with forced-march industrialization was repressed and atomized, deprived of all means of self-expression and terrorized by an omnipresent secret police.

While the Russian experience thus throws little light on the positive side of the problem of constructing socialism, it does provide devastating proof of the impossibility of infusing seemingly socialist forms—such as nationalized means of production and comprehensive economic planning—with genuine socialist content unless the process goes hand-in-hand with the formation of socialist human beings. The idea, assiduously promoted by Soviet ideologists, that raising material living standards of the masses will by itself foster socialist consciousness never had anything to recommend it and has been shown by Soviet (as well as American!) experience to be nonsense. Some of the negative potentialities of the Soviet Russian system were, paradoxically, held in check for a time by the Stalinist terror: a bureaucrat abusing his position too blatantly was likely to find himself in a labor camp, if not worse. But after Stalin's death these restraints were largely removed, and the true nature of the situation was soon revealed.

A recent Chinese critique points to the heart of the matter:

From production to distribution, from economic branches to government organizations, the forces of capitalism run wild in town and countryside. Speculation, cornering the market, price rigging, and cheating are the order of the day: capitalist roaders in enterprises and government team up in grafting, embezzling, working for their own benefit at the expense of the public interest, dividing up the spoils and taking bribes. Socialist ownership by the whole people has degenerated into ownership by a privileged stratum, and is directly manipulated by a handful of capitalist roaders and new bourgeois elements. . . . This has been a painful historical lesson! ("Socialist Construction and Class Struggle in the Field of Economics—Critique of Sun Yeh-fang's Revisionist Economic Theory," by the Writing Group of the Kirin Provincial Revolutionary Committee, *Peking Review*, April 17, 1970, p. 9)

I would stress particularly the statement that "socialist ownership by the whole people has degenerated into ownership by a privileged stratum" with the *caveat* that this is to be interpreted *de facto* rather than *de jure*. It is a privileged stratum—what Charles Bettelheim has called a new "state bourgeoisie"—which controls the means of production and thereby decides how the fruits of production are to be utilized. Regardless of legal forms, this is the real content of class ownership.

It is noteworthy that the foregoing characterization of the situation in the Soviet Union could be applied with little or no change to almost any capitalist country, the main difference being that under capitalism a large part of the activities alluded to are perfectly legal. This underscores the fact that no legal system, using the term in the broadest sense to include the system of property relations, can effectively control men's behavior unless it is in harmony with the historically formed human nature of its subjects. This condition is patently not fulfilled in the Soviet Union.

This of course does not mean that there will never be socialism in the Soviet Union, still less that the failure of the first effort to introduce it has been without positive effects. The earliest appearances of capitalism were also abortive, but they left a precious heritage of experience (including, for example, the invention of double-entry bookkeeping) without which later capitalisms might also have failed or at any rate found development much more difficult. It was through the Russian Revolution that the crucially important science of Marxism-Leninism reached the peoples of Asia, Africa, and Latin America; and it is probably no exaggeration to say that it was only the negative example of later Soviet experience which enabled other countries to see the necessity of protracted revolutionizing practice to the building of socialism. "The restoration of capitalism in the Soviet Union and certain other socialist countries," said Lin Piao on the fiftieth anniversary of the October Revolution, "is the most important lesson to be drawn from the last fifty years of the history of the international Communist movement." (Quoted in *Le Monde Weekly*, January 13, 1971, p. 8)

It was not, however, only the negative lesson of Soviet

experience which impelled the Chinese to pioneer a different road to the construction of socialism. The situation in China differed in important respects from that in Russia. For one thing, the Chinese proletariat, though smaller than the Russian, was never seriously plagued by economism. As Mao wrote in 1939, "Since there is no economic basis for economic reformism in colonial and semi-colonial China as there is in Europe, the whole proletariat, with the exception of a few scabs, is most revolutionary." (*Selected Works,* Vol. II, p. 324) To this consistently revolutionary force there was added another even larger one formed in the quarter-century-long military struggle against capitalism, feudalism, and imperialism, which culminated in the triumph of the Revolution in 1949. In the words of the editors of *Hongqi* (No. 5, 1964): "Owing to the education and training received in the people's army, millions of ordinary workers and peasants and many students and other intellectuals of petty-bourgeois origin have gradually revolutionized themselves [in thinking and action] and become steadfast, politically conscious fighters and mainstays in revolution and construction." (The square brackets are in the original text.) The prolonged civil war in China combined with the war against the Japanese invaders thus fostered a vast growth in both the size and the maturity of the revolutionary forces, while a much shorter period of civil war and resistance to foreign invaders in the Soviet Union seriously weakened the revolutionary forces there. The result was that China, on the morrow of the Revolution, was much more richly endowed with revolutionary human material than Russia had been. Finally, in Lenin and Mao Tse-tung Russia and China were fortunate to have two of the greatest revolutionary geniuses of all time; but Lenin died before the process of constructing socialism had really begun, while Mao's leadership has already lasted more than two decades since the victory of the Revolution.

Both men were well aware of the enormous difficulty of the task that lay ahead after the overthrow of the old regime. In his "Report at the Second All-Russia Trade Union Congress" (January 20, 1919), Lenin said:

The workers were never separated by a Great Wall of China from the old society. And they have preserved a good deal of the traditional mentality of capitalist society. The workers are building a new society without themselves having become new people, or cleansed of the filth of the old world; they are still standing up to their knees in that filth. We can only dream of cleaning the filth away. It would be utterly utopian to think this could be done all at once. It would be so utopian that in practice it would only postpone socialism to kingdom come.

No, that is not the way we intend to build socialism. We are building while still standing on the soil of capitalist society, combating all those weaknesses and shortcomings which also affect the working people and which tend to drag the proletariat down. There are many old separatist habits and customs of the small holder in this struggle, and we still feel the effects of the old maxim: "Every man for himself, and the devil take the hindmost." (*Collected Works*, Vol. 28, 424-425)

Mao was even more explicit when he wrote, as the Peoples Liberation Army was about to win its final victories in March of 1949:

To win country-wide victory is only the first step in a long march of ten thousand *li*. Even if this step is worthy of pride, it is comparatively tiny; what will be more worthy of pride is yet to come. After several decades, the victory of the Chinese people's democratic revolution, viewed in retrospect, will seem like only a brief prologue in a long drama. A drama begins with a prologue, but the prologue is not the climax. The Chinese revolution is great, but the road after the revolution will be longer, the work greater and more arduous. (*Selected Works*, Vol. IV, p. 374)

After only two decades we can see how right Mao was. The drama has continued to unfold, moving from one climax to another. Despite all its initial advantages, China has never been free of the danger of slipping back into the old forms and relations which for centuries had molded Chinese human nature. The old "ensemble of social relations" continued and still continues to exist in the minds and consciousness of hundreds of millions of Chinese. As Marx expressed it in *The Eighteenth Brumaire*, "The tradition of all the dead generations weighs like a nightmare on the brain of the living." (*Werke*, Vol. 8, p. 115) To overcome this ineluctable fact—

not to nationalize property or build heavy industry or raise material living standards, important though all these things are—is the central problem of the transition to socialism. And it was the Chinese revolutionaries under the inspired leadership of Mao Tse-tung who grasped and internalized this truth to the extent of making it the conscious basis of their revolutionizing practice.

This is not the occasion for an attempt to analyze this revolutionizing practice, nor do I have the knowledge and competence which would be required. What I wish to emphasize is that *for the first time* the problem has been fully recognized and correctly posed. Until that was done, there was not even a chance of finding a satisfactory solution.

It is as well to close on a note of caution. In politics, as in science, the first step in solving a problem is to recognize and pose it correctly. But the first step is usually a long way from the final solution, and when the problem is nothing less than changing human nature this *caveat* is doubly and triply relevant. Fortunately, Mao knows this better than anyone else, and we can hope that the knowledge will become a permanent part of his legacy to the Chinese people. Ultimate success or failure will probably not be known until all of us are long since gone and forgotten. Said Mao in 1967 at the height of the Cultural Revolution:

The present Great Proletarian Cultural Revolution is only the first of its kind. In the future such revolutions must take place. . . . All Party members and the population at large must guard against believing . . . that everything will be fine after one, two, three, or four cultural revolutions. We must pay close attention, and we must not relax our vigilance. (Quoted in the concluding chapter of Jean Daubier, *Histoire de la révolution culturelle prolétarienne en Chine* [Paris: Maspero, 1970])

All history, Marx said, is the continuous transformation of human nature. What is Mao telling us but that even after the overthrow of class domination the positive task of transforming human nature never ceases?